Copyright © 2019 by Constantin Obreja

All rights reserved. No part of this publication may be reproduced, distributed, or transmitted in any form or by any means, including photocopying, recording, or other electronic or mechanical methods, without the prior written permission of the publisher, except in the case of brief quotations embodied in critical reviews and certain other noncommercial uses permitted by copyright law. For permission requests, write to the publisher.

TABLE OF CONTENTS

COPYRIGHT

TABLE OF CONTENTS

AFFILIATE MARKETING

HOW TO BECOME AN AFFILIATE MARKETER

WHAT TO SELL ONLINE: 8 STRATEGIES TO FIND YOUR FIRST PRODUCT.

HOW TO FIND PROFITABLE PRODUCTS

WHY AFFILIATE MARKETING IS PROFITABLE ESSENTIAL TIPS FOR BLOGGERS WHO START AFFILIATE MARKETING

AMAZON ASSOCIATES: HOW TO CHOOSE AND PROMOTE THE MOST PROFITABLE PRODUCTS

STEPS TO ATTRACT AFFILIATES TO YOUR PRODUCTS

GETTING STARTED WITH AFFILIATE MARKETING

THE SECRETS OF AFFILIATE MARKETING

WHICH SOCIAL NETWORK TO CHOOSE TO ADVERTISE YOUR BUSINESS?

WHY YOU SHOULD USE SOCIAL MEDIA

HOW TO CHOOSE THE RIGHT AFFILIATE PROGRAM TO PROMOTE

AFFILIATE MARKETING

Affiliation is a partnership between a provider of traffic and a commercial site seeking to develop its activity. The commercial site, then named Announcer proposes a program of affiliation to the site wishing to make profitable its traffic, then named Affiliate. The affiliate program describes how the affiliate will be compensated by promoting the advertiser's products or services. The modes of remuneration can be varied, it is most often:

1. Percentage pay: This percentage, calculated on the total amount of the sale, is paid back to the affiliate who generates it.

2. A fixed remuneration: This fixed amount is paid to the affiliate as soon as he generates a lead, for example a quote request, or a subscription to a newsletter.

3. Pay per click: A fixed amount will be paid to the affiliate for each click generated to the advertiser's site.

Affiliate marketing is a form of paid performance marketing where an affiliate sells items on behalf of a merchant for an agreed rate or percentage of the sale. This is an excellent form of advertising for e- commerce shops since funds are only exchanged after a sale is over, but it works for all business models. As long as you have a product for sale, or can find a product to promote, you can participate in affiliate marketing. What distinguishes this form of marketing is that it benefits all concerned. On the customer side, they are able to find products they may not have found on their own and to gain the approval of someone they (likely) trust. Some advertisers have their own affiliate program, such as Amazon, eBay or Airbnb for example. Others go through external affiliate platforms such as Awin, Commission Junction, Spicyoffers, or Tradedoubler, which have tracking technology and a base of affiliates already active on other programs.

An affiliate program provides affiliates with text links, banners, and product catalogs. Product catalogs are used by price comparison affiliates and affiliates of re-targeting. When multiple affiliates have been involved in a sale, the affiliate service assigns the sale to one of the affiliates based on the rules set by the advertiser. In general, this is last click attribution: The affiliate site that generated the last click is assigned the sale, and therefore the commission. A system that, at its best, works for everyone involved and brings more products to more customers. Affordable and extensive, affiliate marketing is an excellent choice for anyone who wants to increase their bottom line. Whether you are the seller or the merchant. None of this tells you exactly how affiliate marketing works. To understand this, one has to dig into the relationships involved in affiliate marketing.

What are the relationships in affiliate marketing?

Affiliate marketing is all about relationships forged between people. The relationship between the customer and the affiliate must be based on the same basis as the relationship between the affiliate and the merchant: solid trust, fair conditions and transparency. Transparency is not just a suggestion, by the way. It is a legal requirement in the United States. In the purest version of affiliate marketing, there are three parties involved:

1. The customer (public)

2. The affiliate (promoter)

3. The merchant (owner)

With affiliate marketing representing up to 16% of all ecommerce sales, this cycle represents the main process from an affiliate's perspective. First, the affiliate finds a product and connects with the merchant behind him. Then, the affiliate and the merchant agree on a given commission rate - either a flat fee or a percentage - when the affiliate makes sales on behalf of the merchant. Affiliates then promote the product to their audience, often using a special link promotion campaign to track their sales and referrals. Once the transaction is over, the merchant hands over the commission.

An affiliate program is usually public, and affiliates apply to the program. The advertiser then allows the affiliate to relay the program, if it is in line with its selection criteria. Remuneration can vary from one affiliate to another, depending on the sector of activity and the importance of the affiliate. In general, affiliates bringing a large volume of conversions get better pay. The advertiser must also animate its program to make it attractive: challenges rewarding the best affiliates or temporary increases in commissioning are thus frequently used. On an affiliate program, advertisers provide affiliates advertising visuals, catalogs produced in different formats (XML, txt, csv) or communicate how to rewrite their URLs to redirect the user to the page of the advertiser and be able to register it, for affiliates to integrate on their site. When a conversion is recorded, it is not directly remunerated to the affiliate. To avoid fraud, the sale is pending, and the advertiser must subsequently validate this sale. Affiliates receive their commissions with more or less delay, based on the statements of the advertisers. Between a click and a conversion (registration of a lead or a sale), there is loss. The conversion ratio of visitors to buyers is very low, rarely more than 1% on average. However, affiliation is an effective marketing performance tool and allows the advertiser to gain visibility by limiting costs. There is still very little accurate data on the affiliation market in Europe. SRI (Union governed internet) regularly publishes figures for advertising expenditure on the Internet: the first half of 2010, the affiliation accounted for 8% of advertising spending on the Internet, making membership the 4th type of internet advertising investment France behind directories (20%), "display" (22%) and "search" (37%).

History of Affiliation

For Internet affiliation, the story begins in the mid-1990s. The web begins to develop and the first commercial sites appear.

Amazon version

The story, as it is often told, would like Amazon to be at the origin of the concept. The site had even proclaimed, for a while, in the American version of the FAQs of its affiliate program. So initially, according to legend, the idea came from Jeff Bezos, the founder of Amazon. During a cocktail, he met a woman who had expressed his wish to sell books on divorce on his website dedicated to the subject. As a result of this discussion, Jeff Bezos had the idea to suggest to him to insert on his site links to the books in question on Amazon and to be remunerated by a commission for each sale made. And so was born, in July 1996, the affiliate program of the Amazon site. The exchange was simple: advise our books to your visitors and you will receive a commission if they buy. Starting in the year 2000, pure players have systematically opened affiliate programs, usually through a platform. It was not until the resumption of investment on the internet in 2004 to see the arrival of major brands in the world of affiliation.

The unofficial version

The other version is more controversial, because as is the case for many innovations in the web marketing industry, the concept of affiliation was born and appeared for the first time, in the early 1990s, in the world. X industry on the web. To increase the traffic and therefore the turn over of e-commerce sites, some merchants have proposed to webmasters whose sites were well positioned on the search engines to display their products in exchange for a commission on sales generated. Other sites use the purchase of sponsored links to generate traffic on their own site before returning it to the sites of advertisers. Still others form the basis of hundreds of thousands of subscribers to their newsletters, to whom they relay the promotional offers of advertisers.

For the record, the site CyberErotica would be known to be the first site, or one of the first, to have set up an affiliate program. At the time, it was a cost-per-click (CPC) program. Webmasters were paid for each visitor "sent" to the site. Adopted by other sites of the site of the sector at the same time, it was gradually abandoned because of the rate too much fraud to the click. The sites of the porn industry then very quickly turned to the model of the Cost per Sale (CPS), commissioning the affiliates for each sale or subscription generated.

HOW YOU CAN BECOME AN AFFILIATE MARKETER

let's talk about your place in affiliate marketing. If you are a blogger, you have the choice. The larger your audience, the more opportunities there are. But you do not have to be too tall. In fact, a smaller audience has put you in the category of "micro-influencers", and companies love micro-influencers. Micro-influencers deliver better engagement and lower cost than larger-scale influencers. You can build yourself in one year, as the example we looked at earlier demonstrated, but you could be in the game for five years and never make a single affiliate income if you did not seek and identified your niche. Shrinking your niche should be the next step after creating your WordPress blog site.

- **Step 1: Join a network or partner program**

Or, start yours. I will mention a few networks you can join. If you prefer not to follow this path - I understand - you can find partner programs with a quick search.

What is your niche? Use it to find potential programs you can sign up for. For example, if you are putting together a beauty blog, you might want to start with the cosmetics vendors. First, choose the well-known names to see if they have a program for you. The same process would apply for both food blogs and travel blogs. Whatever your niche, use it to find relevant programs, apply for a partnership, and move on to the next step.

- **Step 2: Choose the relevant products**

It's not because a reseller fits your niche that every product will suit you. You have to work on selling these products to earn a commission, so it's important to find products that will resonate with your audience. For example, your niche would probably be much smaller than "women's beauty products". If you sell beauty products from abroad, you would like to find affiliate goodies that meet this criteria.

Cost-effective and relevant products are the key to getting sales pages that look like this:

- High conversion and sales rates

It's even better if it's a product you personally believe in and can vouch for. Becky Mollenkamp, an online entrepreneur and small business owner, has earned hundreds of dollars in recent months through her advocacy of a product she truly believes in. Once these two steps are eliminated, this is the hardest part. But now it's time for the scramble and , the promotion.

- **Step 3: Promote the products**

Blogging is a pretty easy way to get started with promoting a product, but it's not as easy as hooking up a product and telling people to buy it. You must produce high quality content (which usually means long form) to make your point. Longer blog posts can take longer, but they can generate up to nine times more leads , so they are worth it for an affiliate. NerdWallet, for example, the bulk of its income from its partnerships. Almost all of their articles, even their evaluations, exceed the 1000 word mark.

NerdWallet

Responsible for affiliate links, but focused on providing a use for the reader - rather than just making sales - this is a great example of how to do well affiliate blogging. It's also a great example of how to use long- tail keywords to drive traffic for your affiliate links . Long-haul keywords like "Best Credit Card 2018" helped an affiliate make $16,433. In the meantime, here's how to find the best of them. First, go to LongTailPro.

LongTailPro

- Scroll down to bring up the menu with the free trial offer, then click on it and register to open an account.
- Once you're done with that, we'll take you to the dashboard.
- Search for long-tail keywords by entering a few keywords in the box provided. In this case, look for keywords related to digital cameras.
- Here are our results. By default, you will see only 20 results or less, but you can change the settings to get more results.
- Keywords related to digital cameras

These are already solid suggestions that give us a clear idea of how to create content for this kind of product, but there is still much to learn from this tool. Sort by volume to see how the competition is comparing.

Keywords sorted by volume

The price of "digital cameras" will be far too high for us to be able to compete with them (as are the other two options), but the competition drops a lot and there is still a decent volume behind that. With mostly organic results and manageable competition, this one could make a long, viable train for someone trying to create content around digital cameras. But that's not all this tool can do. Scroll down to distinguish yourself from your competitors.

Competition analysis

Nice, is not it? Do you have problems with downtime and WordPress? Kinsta is the hosting solution designed to save you time! Although blogging and SEO are our first suggestions for promoting your products, you should take advantage of the benefits of your list of emails and social networks. Twitter marketing is an art in itself, but if you already have an audience, it's worth a try.

- **Step 4: Profit**

It's a little laughable, but after joining a program, finding a product and promoting it, you only have one thing left to do: enjoy it. Affiliate marketing is beautifully simple. At least in theory.

HOW YOU CAN BECOME AN AFFILIATE TRADER

Becoming a merchant in affiliate marketing is a little more difficult than becoming an affiliate, although it shares many of the same steps. If you are already an established e-commerce store, you can skip steps 1 and 2. If this is not the case, go for it thoroughly.

- **Step 1: Identify a niche**

If you remember, affiliate marketing depends on the relationships involved. As a trader, you have an additional relationship to maintain: a relationship with your customers. And if you want to create an affiliate program or e-commerce store that brings more than just change, you need a niche. You will get fewer prospects with a niche market, but a higher conversion rate.

Comparison between general marketing and niche marketing

A mass market can work for some products - like Apple products - but for a store that is interested in generating sales as quickly as possible, a niche is the way to go. It's also vital if you want to work with affiliates who have a lot of influence on an audience. Which means that you are going to need someone who has his own niche of attraction.

You can identify a niche in two ways.

   I. Start with a product.
   II. Start with an audience.

If you have a product you want to sell , you should strive to find a market need for that product from a specific audience. Instead of looking at demographics like location, look for audiences based on psychographic attributes. After all, 57% of buyers bought from a retailer away from them. If you limit your customers to a locality, you will also limit your funds.

Behaviour of e-commerce users

Examples of psychographic attributes could be hobbies, family life and tax philosophy. The chart below provides a broad breakdown of how this differs from traditional demographic data.

Psychography vs demography

So if you were trying to sell a product like an online finance course, your audience might have psychographic features like:

- Lower levels of financial literacy. Owners of small businesses or start-ups. Order values. If the product you want to sell meets the needs of people with these attributes, you've found the audience you should be addressing. If this is not the case, you must continue to search. Note that most e-commerce stores follow the second pattern - starting with the public - and then find a product, using the same market needs parameters.
- The specific circumstances in which you can start with a product are when you create something unique and new, in which case your goal will be to create demand rather than respond to it.

Step 2: Create the terms of your affiliate program

We talked about the need to offer competitive commission rates. Generally, your commission rate should start at 10%. But to get off to a good start, look at your competitors to set your affiliate commission rates. What do they offer? See if you can offer better. Affiliates need to go to work selling your product - creating social media articles, blogs, hosting webinars, and so on - so it must be worth it. In addition, clarify your conditions from the beginning. The higher your commission rate, the better. This will help you eliminate people who want too much and save time for both parties by keeping everyone on the same page. When we started our own affiliate system , which is very good and offers the highest payments in the industry, we have kept that in mind. Specifically, for each Kinsta hosting plan, you receive a unique sign-up bonus:

- If someone you recommend fits the Starter plan, you get $ 50.
- If someone you recommend fits on the Pro plan, you get $ 100.
- If someone you recommend fits one of the Business Plans, you get $ 150.
- If someone you recommend is enrolled in one of the Business Plans, you get $ 500.
- Affiliates receive a recurring monthly fee of 10% for each sponsorship, in addition to the sign-up bonus.

But if you also think I'm not objective, I can tell you that BigCommerce is a good example to follow as well:

BigCommerce Affiliate Program

Other terms to consider with your own affiliate program include:

- Whether it is a single payment or recurring revenue (as in the case of a subscription service).
- Whether to create assets for your program such as banners, social media templates and logos. I know it takes more time and resources, but the more you give affiliates something to work with, the easier it is for them to sell on your behalf.

- Whether to set up with an affiliate platform or a WordPress extension. Rewardful is a particularly easy-to-use platform for a novice affiliate marketer.

Competitive price

Once you have defined your terms, post them on an easy-to-find page of your site - most people keep their links in the footer - and attach a contact form. Then promote it to your blog, social channels and your site. Then, optimize for search engines. Or, if you prefer a more proactive approach, go to step three.

Step 3: Find the relevant influencers

Letting affiliates find you is an easy way to navigate, but if your business is brand new, you will not interact anytime soon. So instead, you have to go see them. One of the easiest - and cheapest - ways to find relevant influencers is to search for blogs in your niche. Start by entering a long-tail keyword like "Financial Advice for Small Businesses" via Google.

Here's what you get :

- Search query

Then follow the links and look for a "partner with us", "work with us" or "advertise" page. The first result gives us this in the footer.

- Finder.com

Going down, we land on their partnership page with their conditions, which are not bad:

- So what should you do now? Fill in your information and start the conversation. Repeat this process until you have gathered a handful of affiliates you trust.
- As they increase your audience for you, your own affiliate page should start to see some momentum too. Which means that our last step is quite simple.

Step 4: Profit (again)

Just like an affiliate, your last step as a trader is to enjoy your hard work. Track your sales with your extensions or continue to expand your product offering and support your affiliates with fast payments. After all, if you treat them well, they will become your best sellers. And these are people who deserve to be encouraged, right?

WHAT TO SELL ONLINE: 8 STRATEGIES TO FIND YOUR FIRST PRODUCT.

For new entrepreneurs, deciding to set up your e-commerce business is exciting, but it's also a new field that can be intimidating and difficult to navigate. One of the biggest challenges aspiring entrepreneurs face is knowing what to sell online - whether it's a single product or several products that occupy a niche in a market. Finding new ideas can be difficult, and you often have the impression that everything has already been done; not to mention the fierce competition that exists today. Consumers are just a few clicks away from online e-commerce giants like Amazon, Walmart, Zappos and Best Buy, which are extremely difficult to compete on search engines. But there are still golden opportunities, and new products that are very successful are being marketed very frequently.

So, how can you take action? We have listed eight strategies and opportunities that you can use to generate product ideas.

Products and Niches: Types of Opportunities

Below you will find a list of eight potential opportunities that can help you find your own product or niche. Each requires a different approach and state of mind.

- Find keyword opportunities
- Create an interesting / captivating brand
- Identify a point of pain
- Identify the passions of the customers
- Follow your own passion
- Look for an untapped market opportunity
- Consider your experience
- Enjoy a trend beginning

Let's analyse each opportunity in more detail:

1. Find keyword opportunities

It is well known that organic search traffic is a powerful marketing channel. Searching for keyword opportunities involves strategic research that is based on the search queries most used by users, as well as the volume of searches and competition for these keywords. This approach is quite technical and requires a good knowledge in the areas of SEO and keyword research. The fact of finding opportunities of keywords can be a strategic way to capture traffic consisting from Google. This strategy is especially useful if you plan to sell your products in dropshipping because the margins of products sold in dropshipping are very low, which makes it very difficult to use paid advertising channels.

Example: When Andrew Youderian had just started e-commerce, his goal was to build a business that would generate profit and provide him with flexibility. For this reason, the viability of his business was much more important to him than being passionate about the product he was selling. Therefore, he followed a technical approach to choosing a niche in which he really thought he had a chance of succeeding, basing the selection of his niche on a meticulous keyword search. Andrew Youderian has found a way to rank well for keywords in the fishing equipment industry and in the CB radio niche.

2. Build an Interesting and Unique Brand

The opportunity to build a brand requires a very different approach to that outlined above for SEO. It often involves a better understanding of your customers, and the development of a unique brand to occupy a special place in the minds of your customers. A brand building approach can be particularly effective in differentiating you if margins are too low or competition is fierce.

Examples: Dbrand manufactures pouches for smartphones, laptops and game consoles. In just over a year, dbrand team members have been able to build their brand to reach 64,000 fans on Facebook, thanks to their truly unique customer communication culture. Tapping into the same culture, using reddit, and adding a unique sense of humor catapulted dbrand to the top of the industry.

To create a successful brand, you will need to choose a product or area of activity that allows you to position yourself in a new or unique way. An example of a successful business is DODOcase, an iPad case manufacturing company. DODOcase operates in a very competitive and almost saturated space. However, his cases are hand-crafted with traditional craft binding techniques in the city of San Francisco. And if it's something you want, you can only buy it from Dodocase.

3. Identify a "Pain Point" at the Client

Solving a pain point at the customer has always been a good way to make sales. Tylenol could not have maintained her activities if the migraine did not hurt. A pain point does not have to refer to physical pain, but can also refer to frustrating or unpleasant experiences.

Example : Jing understood that people had unpleasant pain when grinding their teeth. Not only physical, since over time, chronic teeth grinding may require several visits to the dentist, with often high bills. Knowing it was a pain point, that people would naturally look for a solution to solve it, and that they would spend money without hesitation, he created Pro Teeth Guard . Pro Teeth Guard is a company that manufactures personalized mouthguards to prevent grinding of teeth during sleep.

Active Hound is another very good example of a brand that has solved a point of pain in the market. After talking with other dog owners at the local park, the founders discovered a major dissatisfaction among these owners; Dog toys are very expensive and do not last long. Understanding this has inspired them to create a sustainable range of dog toys that are highly resistant to chewing, and even to slightly muscular games. Take a minute to think about the pain and annoyances of your everyday life, it may help you find your next great product idea.

4. Identify Customer Passions

Serving your clients' passions is as good or maybe even better than pain points. When customers are passionate about something, they will often spend more money. Golfers are well known for spending thousands of dollars to lower their handicap by just one point. Additional benefits of this approach may include deeper interaction with your brand and greater loyalty to it; since passionate customers are generally more involved in the industry and in the buying process.

Example: Black Milk Clothing is a company started in 2009, following the explosion of "TooManyTights", the blog community of the founders. By noticing the passion and opportunity in the niche of women's tights, they created Black Milk Clothing. Today, Black Milk is a multi-million dollar company that employs over 150 people and distributes its products globally. They do an excellent job of integrating an aspect of pop culture into their designs, allowing them to reach passionate audiences and customers in different markets.

5. Follow Your Passion

Some people think that the fact choosing a niche according to one's own passion can lead to disaster. This is not always the case, and it can even be very profitable. Creating an e-commerce business requires a lot of effort, and you will surely encounter some difficulties on your way. Passion is often what allows you to persist during difficult times. For some people, the passion to build a business may be enough to drive them to succeed, but it is usually essential that you are as passionate about the products you sell and your industry. Staying motivated is essential to building and running an e-commerce business in difficult times. It is said that if you love what you do, you will never have to work another day of your life.

Example: Eric Bandholz started BeardBrand as a blog dealing with the business world and sales strategies. Slowly, his passion for beards became prominent in his discussions. Over time, he turned his passion for the bearded lifestyle into a thriving e-commerce business selling beard care products.

Moorea Seal is another example of a person who turned his passion into a thriving e-commerce business. In 2010, Moorea, a full-time artist living in Seattle, became self-employed to focus on her creative activities that include: blogging, managing her jewelry business, illustration, and graphic design. At the end of 2012, she retired early from the design world to devote more time to her passions and focus on her personal activities. In 2013, Moorea opened a store on Shopify. The Moorea Seal boutique offers a fine selection of beautiful accessories and objects, highlighting those handcrafted by US-based artists. Each of the designers was deliberately and carefully chosen by Moorea herself, and 7% of the store's revenue goes to non-profit organizations that are very important to him. The Moorea Seal Shop has been very successful in less than a year, and has been featured in several blogs and publications, including The Huffington Post, Design Sponge and Babble.

6. Consider Your Experience

Have you ever worked in a particular industry and know it from the ground up? Maybe you have a skill or set of experiences that make you an expert in a given field? Turning your expertise into your own online business is a very good way to enter the market with an advantage that may not be as easy to replicate by your competitors.

Example: Jonathan Snook is an expert in web design and web development. He took advantage of his years of experience and knowledge to write and self-publish a book on web development and CSS entitled: SMACSS, Evolutive and Modular Architecture for CSS.

Jillian Michael of "The Biggest Loser" used the same approach and used her expertise in fitness and weight loss to develop and sell a range of products, including DVDs, books and fitness equipment.

7. Enjoy a Beginning of Trend

Enjoying trends early can be very exciting for a new company. It makes it possible to find a place in the minds of consumers and to establish itself as a leader before others do it. "Jump" on an early trend can have a big impact on your SEO, and will allow you to climb to the top of the search rankings faster and easier.

Example: Sophie Kovic, founder of Flockstocks, had noticed a trend beginning for feather hair extensions. Before spending money or buying inventory, she tested the market by designing a website very quickly to test. The results ? 11 sales in 4 hours. Knowing that there was a huge opportunity, she created her website, ordered the stock and even ended up winning the "Build a Business" contest from Shopify in 2012 in the category of clothing and jewelry.

Have You Found Your Opportunity?

- Keep in mind that because of the strong competition in the most popular and popular product categories, choosing the right niche can be the key to your success. Do not be afraid to focus on small niches and product categories. Even if a niche is a small subset of a larger category, with fewer potential customers, you will have the benefit of having less competition and a more targeted audience. With less competition, you'll be more likely to climb to the top of Google; and generally, advertising to reach your audience is more efficient and less expensive.
- The niche and products you choose will shape your business as a whole, the activities you will do, and the challenges you will face. For example, the sale of food products is very different from the sale of electronic products or smartphone cases; therefore, you will naturally face different challenges.

- Understanding each of the eight opportunities presented above should help you get into the bath, and find your first niche or product.

HOW TO FIND PROFITABLE PRODUCTS

As a new trader, you need to find products to sell and services to offer. Products on your shelves and those listed on your e-commerce website shape your brand image. The goal is to find products tailored to your business that will appeal to your audience and sell easily. By studying your niche market, you will be able to ensure that your potential products / services will interest your target customers. Which products or services best meet their needs? What added value will a particular product provide to your customers? These are just a few of the questions to ask as part of the product selection process for sale.

Your success will depend on the quality of the research conducted, the main purpose of this research is to help you find a product that meets the needs of a niche market. This is called product-market matching. The choice of products with high profitability potential is thus crucial for both online stores and physical stores. But what do we mean by product-market correspondence and how to evaluate it? We detail the concept in this article so you can take advantage of it in your online or in-store sales activity.

What is product-market matching?

Product-to-market matching is a concept for assessing how well a product meets the needs of a market, or simply the potential for profitability of what you offer. Even without knowing this concept, most retailers instinctively try to find the right product-market match based on their audience - they try to find out what consumers want, offer products for sale that are highly likely to interest them, and what is needed to create a tempting value proposition in order to capture a larger market share. Whether you want to change your brand, change your product selection, or have just started your business, finding products with high profitability potential is often a complex task.

Ask yourself a few questions before starting the decision-making process, including: "What products do I enjoy, buy, and that I find useful?" "Does the sale of this product / service excite me? ". It is very likely that your interest in one product will be shared by other consumers, indicating that there is demand. In addition, you will be more excited about selling a product that you are passionate about and your customers will notice. Even if trendy products can be sold faster, or encourage a new audience to be interested in your brand, it would be difficult to build a lasting brand by selling only the flavour of the month. It is often easier to build a consistent brand by selling mostly timeless products and a few trendy products on appropriate occasions.

Even if it is more practical to first choose products before building a sales activity centered on the offers in question, it is always possible - in the case of an existing company - to replace the products already on sale and to to make your business adapt to changes.

How to find what to sell: identify opportunities

Products that you like and want to discover to consumers, products that fill a demand ignored by your competitors, find the right product-market match often involves the identification of a business opportunity.

1. Explore keyword opportunities: Start with a keyword search for your niche and audience.

2. Build an interesting and exciting brand: Create a unique and interesting brand to sell your products. Identify and solve a point of pain in the consumer.

3. Follow your own passion: Inject your passions and interests into your business and product selection.

4. Identify an untapped market opportunity: Do you want some products? Analyse your potential competitors to see if they offer similar items, or if you could be the first seller to market them. Use your expertise and experience.

5. Take advantage of the trends early: Do you intend to sell trendy products? Make sure you have them in store or list them on your e-commerce site as soon as possible.

Most retailers offer both trendy and mainstream products to ensure consumer satisfaction at all levels - providing consumers with the items they need and the products they would like to buy out of desire.

- Study your customers to choose the right products

In order to be able to choose your niche and focus on an opportunity that can benefit your business, you need to know your audience. If you do not know your customers, it will be difficult to find a good product-market match. By gaining an in-depth knowledge of the problems faced by your customers, you will be able to better understand them, gain their trust and enhance your credibility. You can find out what your audience is interested in by identifying successful industry leader offers, by organizing focus groups or surveys to ask target customers about the products you would like to sell, and by learning more about them. about the interests of your audience.

Even though customers frequently buy consumer goods, they are also willing to invest their money in products / services that solve a problem or that they are passionate about. Comprehensive knowledge of your audience is the key to long-term customer loyalty. Knowing your audience is also crucial, as at the end of the day, once a good product-market match is achieved, your customers will recognize the value of your product and will be willing to promote it to others. Satisfied customers will become loyal promoters of your brand and spread the message. The word of mouth recommendations clearly indicate that it is a good match-market product and your offer provides superior value to your customers.

- Repositioning an existing product

Your existing product does not appeal to customers? If they do not buy it, how should you react? Maybe it does not meet their needs - or it just does not meet the good needs. In this case, you could promote your product in another market where it will be better received to stimulate sales.

Here are some questions to ask yourself:

Is your current market saturated? Do you compete with multiple competitors that prevent you from having a competitive advantage in your niche? Is your product quite different from competing products? Is your value proposition clear enough? Could your product meet needs in a high-end market, where customers are willing to pay more and buy more? Or is it the opposite - would it be better to target more price-sensitive consumers? It is also possible to change the team working on a product, to rename a product or to promote it in a new way, or to use many other tactics until you find a good product-market match.

- Align products with your brand

Once the products you intend to sell selected, it will be important to align your offers with your existing brand. Otherwise, you will need to create a new brand that better reflects the items in question. Whether you sell in-store, at markets, at trade shows, or at festivals, creating a brand identity will be essential. Customers want to know if your product / service will meet their needs. Therefore, it would be wise to inject their needs into the history of your brand. In addition, integrating your product's story with your brand image helps to present a consistent and neat identity to your audience, helping customers to better remember your product offering.

The story of your brand, the cause that it supports, and the product itself merge to form one and the same story. Most customers who buy the products of a particular brand know the history of the particular brand - this is what inspires them and encourages them to repeat their purchases.

- Product-market matching: measuring success

Launch your product smoothly and follow the sales indicators, after identifying the products that best fit your sales activity, make a smooth launch and analyze customer feedback. Start with a test: place a small order, then set a deadline and sales goals. Once 3/4 of the ordered products are sold, analyse the time it took to sell them, the item return rate, and the amount of revenue customers make additional purchases. Although KPIs are different for each brand, be sure to prioritize the time it took to fully sell the new product stock. If most of your sales are done online, you could afford to stock the new products for longer periods of time - the approach to avoid, however, for in-store sales. After all, physical shop windows must constantly showcase new arrivals.

- Examine your point of sale system data

Point of Sale (POS) data will allow you to track your sales and whether to adjust your strategy during the testing phase.

- Follow customer reviews and recommendations

Once customers start buying your product, follow their feedback closely. Do they leave ratings on your website, social pages or customer experience sharing sites like Yelp? Do they encounter difficulties when using the product? Are their needs fully met? In addition to reviews, analyse how often they share information about your product or brand. If they recommend your shop to their surroundings, it is a vote of confidence and a sign indicating excellent product-market correspondence.

In addition to following customer conversations online, have them personally share their stories. Have comment cards near the checkout counter, insert links to surveys in receipts, or send emails to customers to find out if they would recommend your product. These feedbacks will be very useful for refining your market positioning (and will provide you with great ideas on how to promote the product).

WAYS TO SELL MORE AFFILIATE MARKETING PRODUCTS

Are you interested in making money as an affiliate or currently making money as an affiliate and looking to take your earnings to a higher level? In this chapter, you will discover 3 strategies that you can use to increase your affiliate marketing revenue and take your promotional efforts to a higher level. The promotion of affiliate marketing may often want to walk on eggs because you do not want to give the impression that your list of subscribers and readers of your blog are too aggressive or "sellers", even if you have need to be confident and assured to make money. Your goal as a marketing affiliate is to be able to maximize the amount of money you earn, without extinguishing your followers. You want your affiliate promotions to add value to your users' experience.

YouWhat is the best way to achieve my income goals?

Fortunately, the art of promotion is not a big mystery. Much of what you have learned or read about classic "real world" promotion tactics will apply to online affiliate marketing. Let's take a look at the basics:

1. **Promote the affiliate products you use and believe in**

You have to look yourself in the mirror every day and deal with your conscience in order to choose affiliate products that you would buy yourself and recommend to your own friends and family members without hesitation. Before money starts to flow, new affiliate marketers must work hard to establish their credibility. If people trust your opinion and believe in its authenticity, the rest of affiliate marketing, that is, technical details, merchant payments, customer tracking, and so on. If you only recommend good quality products that add value to your followers then you will develop a good reputation and repeat sales of affiliate marketing will be easy.

On the other hand, if you recommend anything and everything that you recommend, you will lose your trust and you will lose long-term followers. That said, ebooks and information products are well suited for beginners in affiliate marketing in this regard. They are relatively cheap all the way (fifty dollars on average in most niches), so buying a personal copy will not waste a lot of time. You are then able to offer an honest opinion about the book and convey your message to the target audience. Sometimes it is possible to contact the merchant directly through your affiliates' page or by other means to request a free review or copy. Some sellers are quite hospitable to beginners, but you should still be ready to explain why you deserve a free product. Talk about your platform, your passion for the niche and how you plan to promote the merchant's merchandise. Quick access to a new merchant's offering may be essential to forming business alliances for the future and beating the competition to increase sales.

2. Describe your personal experiences with the product to your audience

In niches such as nutrition, personal fitness and various sporting hobbies such as fishing, the relationship of personal results from the use of affiliate products will humanize you and help you build rapport with your list. For example, you may have successfully completed a 30-day clean-up strategy from a book; lose 10 pounds and feel better than ever. Talk to your prospects! This will soften the difficult aspects of selling your delivery and convince them that you are the bargain (Note: Show them pictures or screenshots 'before' and 'after' if you have them).

In short, your product evaluations will be more convincing and authentic, and you will have more material to use as list content (email series) and bonus options thereafter. This type of affiliate promotion case study is the most effective way to promote the product, just share your trip and your results. You do not need to use the products yourself to promote the products as an affiliate. You can also share the experiences of others.

3. Select the promotion methods adapted to your platform

Affiliate marketers have many promotional tactics at their disposal, and often test several of them for a given campaign. Some of the most popular methods include:

- Promotion by email to your contact list
- Use of social networks (eg Facebook, LinkedIn, Twitter)
- Product Reviews
- Premiums Advertising banners.

Each of these methods has its strengths and weaknesses, and the selection is often based on personal preferences, past results and actual tests. You should start with methods that meet your needs or strengths. The best way to start is to focus only on one or more methods of promotion and master these methods before adding other methods of promotion. If you try to learn and do everything at the same time, you will scatter too much and you will not get momentum with a particular method to reach your audience and generate traffic. For beginners, one of the best ways to get started is email marketing and listing because it's a proven way to attract "fans" who will "know, love and trust you" and who will finally be happy to buy products on your links. Combined with a WordPress blog to anchor your promotional efforts, you will be able to build lasting and mutually beneficial relationships.

AFFILIATE MARKETING AND INFLUENCE MARKETING

Affiliate marketing and influence marketing. What type of marketing is best suited to your current business goals? Affiliate marketing and influence marketing are two disciplines used by promoters to suggest or promote products. These two strategies give surprising results in terms of return on investment. But which one should you choose for your strategy? Affiliate marketing or influence marketing: your decision will affect your online marketing strategies.

Differences Between Affiliate Marketing and Influence Marketing

The influence of marketing refers to the process of identifying key people with a strong presence on networks and taking advantage of their influence on followers (or subscribers) to promote products or services.

The influencers are bloggers, journalists, authors, consultants, analysts, etc. The most useful influencers usually have:

- Strong influence on potential customers A major reach towards your audience on your website and a significant presence on social networks;The ability to transmit strong links with the brand;
- The credibility and trust of their audience as specialists in their field.

Influencers can help brands build brand awareness and public engagement because their followers trust their recommendations. In affiliate marketing, on the other hand, a company associates with affiliates (bloggers, publishers, companies, organizations, etc.) to promote its brand. In both cases, the same goal is pursued; how different are these two types of marketing? In which cases do you prefer one to the other? Here are 5 factors to consider before making a decision:

1. Study your target audience

This is one of the most important aspects to guide your choice between affiliate marketing and influence marketing. Affiliates can help your products reach your ideal audience with links to your company's products or services. However, if you want to make a product known through recommendations, you will have to think about customizing your sale with the help of influencers.

2. New ways of doing marketing

A few years ago, affiliate marketing was in its infancy. Software today allows companies to go further than ever. Like influence marketing, affiliate marketing has thrived through social networks. To know when to prefer one strategy to another is to decide for the long term. Affiliate marketing can be a good strategy for a campaign, while it will be ideal to turn to influencers at another time.

3. Differentiated costs

Affiliates receive a share of the proceeds from the sale they contributed from their website, which is a commission on the sale. This form of compensation makes affiliate marketing one of the most profitable strategies. On the other hand, with influence marketing, influencers perceive a fixed remuneration which depends, among other factors, on the number of followers they have to promote the brand. In addition, influencers can receive products for free in exchange for their promotion. Affiliate programs are primarily designed to attract new customers and, as a result, increase revenue. For the same purpose, influencer marketing tends to focus more on brand awareness.

4. Measures and follow-up

Influencer marketing uses the influencer site and social network analysis to track and measure brand-driven advertising. It uses indicators such as:

- Total Audience: Subscribers, followers, blog traffic, website visits.
- Engagement: Visits, likes, clicks on links, comments, likes and Shares.
- Participations.
- Subscriptions to newsletters.

- New followers on the different spaces of the social networks of the brand.

Affiliate marketing uses tracking cookies and a pixel placed on the brand's site to track and measure response-driven advertising. These measures are generally more accurate and can allow a more reliable return on investment calculation for the brand. This includes:

- Registration, email signatures, prize draws, sales, orders, subscriptions.
- Percentage of conversion.
- New customer & loyal customer.
- Average value of the order.
- Cost Per Acquisition (CPA).
- Customer value (CLV).

5. Disadvantages of both strategies

However, affiliate marketing and influence marketing do not go without a number of disadvantages, such as:

A- Awards

The Federal Trade Commission (FTC), the US advertising law enforcement agency, has started cracking down on brands that reward bloggers, publishers, or those who advertise their products and services, without making any claims. these rewards. In influencer marketing, the compensation received from brands for promoting their products is often not disclosed.

Another problem for brands working with influencers is to make sure they are working properly for their pay. This factor also affects the choice between affiliate marketing and influence marketing.

B.- Rules

Most unaffiliated influencers are unaware of the basic rules of disclosure, do not understand or care about them. In affiliate marketing, the process of administration and supervision is much more structured, to verify that affiliates are distributing the publications ; a well-managed program also involves affiliate program managers to ensure the application of what they do.

For example, if an affiliate does not systematically reveal that he will receive a commission if his readers make a purchase through his site, the affiliate program administrator may remove it from the program. That said, Google has recently started cracking down on publishers, influencers and affiliates by asking them to make sure that every link to a provider is labeled "nofollow" in their HTML code and that any relationship with a brand is clear. This is a noticeable difference between affiliate marketing and influence marketing.

HOW TO PROMOTE A PRODUCT ONLINE

You have found a product for sale online and created your e-commerce store. And now? Once everything is in place, it's time to start driving traffic to your store and closing sales. Whether you're looking to make your first sale online or have an existing e-commerce business, it's always good to discover new ways to promote your products online.

How to promote a product: 19 creative ideas to test

Here are 19 creative ideas to promote a new product or existing product in your online store. Review the different techniques presented below, and test the ones that you think are most promising.

1. Gift guides

What do you do when you struggle to find a gift idea? If you're like most people, you're probably looking for inspiration on Google. You then review all the gift guides that appear in the search results. Why not include your own product in these gift guides? There are some in all niches, for all types of occasions, and for all types of profiles. Take note of the guides that appear in the first pages of the results and contact the publishers who publish them to see if you could be included. These guides could become a great source of traffic for your online store.

Keep in mind that you will need to provide a compelling reason for your product to be put forward. The author or publisher of the guide should feel that adding your product will enrich their publication - so be sure to highlight the strengths of what you are offering.

2. Marketing by e-mail

E-mail is one of the most effective customer acquisition channels. And while other channels like organic search require some time to generate traffic, e-mail marketing can produce immediate results. That's why you should rely on email marketing to promote your e-commerce site. No need to spend all your time writing and sending e-mails. Simplify your life by configuring a series of automated e-mail campaigns designed to increase your revenue. There are several possibilities:

- Send an e-mailing campaign to encourage new subscribers to take advantage of an attractive offer.
- Send an e-mailing campaign to present additional products to customers who have just made their first purchase and thank them for their support.
- Send an e-mailing campaign to recover the abandoned baskets and encourage prospects to finalize their order.

3. Affiliate programs

If you are struggling to make sales and you do not have enough budget to hire marketing assistants, consider offering an affiliate program on your online store. Affiliate marketing programs allow third-party sellers to promote your product in exchange for a commission. You only pay these if they make a sale. As part of your affiliate program, you will need to create a custom URL for each vendor who promotes your products. These partners could for example share their link on social networks, in a blog article where your product is evaluated, or even in a YouTube video where your article is presented. Thanks to the personalized links, you will be able to follow the sales they make and pay them their commissions.

Know that you will need to train your affiliates to effectively promote your products. Remember: Since affiliates are trying to sell your products for you, you might consider that they are your own dedicated marketing team. If you do not provide them with a list of good practices to follow, you will make it more difficult for them and they will be forced to improvise.

4. Create partnerships with the media

It's thanks to good media coverage that you will be able to reach new customers and allow more people to discover your product. Well-known journalists are inundated with press releases and requests for collaboration. Maximize your chances by targeting ezines instead.

Instead of sending press releases to magazine publishers, send them a personalized e-mail asking if they would like to receive a sample. You can target different publications in your niche and magazines focused on curating products.

Recommended reading : Online media coverage: how to benefit from it for free .

5. Live Broadcasts with Periscope

Although Periscope is still a relatively new social platform, its marketing potential has been clearly demonstrated. Several e-merchants are already known through this live broadcast service by publishing very short videos - instead of sharing such tweets or Facebook updates. You can use Periscope in several ways to promote a product. For example, you could use Periscope to demo a product, answer questions during a QR session, and even take your fans behind the scenes to immerse themselves in the world of your business.

6. Pinterest

Pinterest is a platform that is particularly suitable for selling products online. 93% of active Pinterest users say they use the platform to plan purchases. Not surprisingly, many people use Pinterest to create wish lists. All of these reasons make it a great place to promote products - especially when it comes to well-designed products that allow you to take beautiful photos.

The Pinterest pins also have the advantage of having a long life. It is not uncommon for pins to be consulted months after publication. Take a strategic approach by publishing your pins at peak times when the volume of connected users is important, choosing relevant keywords, and using compelling images. You could even hold contests on the platform to expand your reach.

7. Pinterest Enriched Pins

You can take your Pinterest marketing to the next level with rich pins. This feature allows you to display additional information that is very relevant to your pins. Among the 4 types of enriched pins that exist, it is the pins enriched with products that will be most useful to optimize and streamline the shopping experience. Product-enhanced pins let you display the price of your item in real time, indicate availability, and specify where it can be purchased.

8. Custom Facebook Audiences

Billions of people use Facebook, and as an advertising platform, Facebook provides advanced targeting options for paid advertising. In particular, it is possible to effectively promote an online product through the functionality of Facebook Custom Audiences. This feature allows you to show your ads to visitors to your website and subscribers by email when they are connected to their

Facebook account. These ads tend to perform very well since you know exactly who you are targeting and can customize your ads accordingly.

9. Facebook Shop section

You can further optimize your Facebook marketing by adding a Shop section to your Facebook page. This feature allows users to discover your offers more easily. Your Facebook store will redirect users to your website where they can finalize their purchase.

If you are a Shopify merchant, you can set up the creation of your Facebook store directly in Shopify. This will give users and fans the opportunity to learn more about your products, view your images, and purchase your items once they are redirected to your website.

10. Search Engine Optimization

Even if you have to be patient, organic search provides one of the few possibilities to create a sustainable source of qualified traffic. Creating an effective SEO strategy involves several steps, including developing a relevant content strategy, researching and studying keywords, optimizing site architecture and performance (eg create category pages, increase loading speed), and build a quality feedback links profile.

Although the work to be done is huge, the avalanche effect will quickly take over to make your job easier. If you have already established a basic SEO strategy and want to take things to the next level, we recommend you check out the following resource: Guide to searching for e-commerce keywords.

11. Uncrate

Uncrate is a state-of-the-art curation site that has a very important loyal audience. People who attend Uncrate do not just do it to discover innovative products, they also like to buy them. If your product is featured on Uncrate, you will maximize your chances of generating sales, gaining new leads, and getting noticed by other potential collaborators along the way.

It is not easy to be presented on Uncrate. There is no formal process to follow, but one thing is certain: your product must be very forward thinking to be retained by the editorial team. Some startups were discovered by the Uncrate team, but other entrepreneurs managed to partner with the magazine by submitting an application or sending a sample.

12. Sponsorship Marketing

Sponsorship marketing, also known as word of mouth marketing, is one of the oldest marketing techniques. Sponsorship marketing depends on your ability to get people talking about your product to increase brand awareness and boost sales. Nowadays, it is possible to rely on the Web to multiply the effectiveness of sponsorship marketing. In addition to allowing you to reach more people, the Web also makes it easy for people to share your content and track the impact.

13. Making contact with bloggers

It is difficult to launch a new activity to promote a product without having already built its audience. In this case, you have to either pay to generate traffic, or rely on other people's audiences to build your own community. By partnering with bloggers, you can maximize the appeal of your product and reach potential customers more easily. You do not lose anything by asking reputable bloggers to present your product. If they have an engaged audience and are open to partnerships, you could be generating a lot of traffic and sales.

14. Advertising on Reddit

While most e-merchants are not yet thinking of using them, Reddit ads can be very effective. Sometimes the least used advertising channels are the most profitable because of the low cost and the ability to differentiate more easily. Test advertising on Reddit to promote your product. You can create a sponsored publication that shows your e-commerce site in sub-reddit. Take the opportunity to highlight your product and offer a discount. Make sure your publication is naturally one of the other sub-reddit messages in question.

15. Blog posts

Blogging is a great way to promote your online store. By following the right approach, blogging can be an effective way to generate traffic and associate a lifestyle with your products. The results of a study conducted by HubSpot have shown that it is possible to increase its traffic by publishing more blog articles.

Use your own blog to drive traffic and promote your products. Implemented correctly, blogging can drive search engine traffic, attract customers, and capture the attention of reputable media and bloggers who might decide to write about you.

16. Instagram

The Instagram network has more than 400 million active users, and being focused on photo sharing makes it an ideal platform for promoting products. Half of these users connect to Instagram every day. Any brand could increase the appeal for its products by establishing a presence on this network.

There are many ways to use Instagram to promote an e-commerce store. You could share captivating photos of your products, a stop motion video to display one of your products in action, organize a quiz, or contact influential accounts on Instagram to offer to present your product in a sponsored publication. .

17. YouTube

The YouTube platform is also one of the most used search engines to find new content. In addition, YouTube videos may also appear in the results of regular search engines like Google. This represents a huge traffic opportunity.

No need to create a viral video to get results on YouTube. You can really promote your products through informative or interesting videos. Many consumers may already be searching for your products or brand on YouTube. By creating a professional channel that hosts your own videos, you can control the story.

18. Organize a contest

Contests are an effective way to reach a large audience and increase brand awareness. By offering your product as a contest prize, you will be sure to attract qualified participants - ie. potential prospects. That said, several quizzes fail. There are some mistakes to avoid when organizing a contest to promote your brand. Make sure the platform, timing, message, and steps to enter the contest are well thought out.

19. Bonus: Ephemeral Boutiques

Even if you run an online business, you can enjoy the benefits of physical selling without opening a permanent store and take the opportunity to promote your e-commerce site in person while selling your product in the physical world. There are certainly unused spaces in your city that you could rent for a week - or even a weekend - to open an ephemeral shop.

By opening an ephemeral shop, you will be able to present some of your products in exclusivity, get noticed by the local press, take advantage of the craze for periods of intense shopping, and talk with customers in person to better understand them.

GETTING STARTED WITH AFFILIATE MARKETING

Affiliate marketing is one of the main tools of Internet marketing, that is, promoting certain goods or services of other companies and obtaining a percentage of sales. Affiliate marketing provides businesses with new ways to market their products and increase sales . Companies are willing to pay for those who help promote their products. This type of cooperation is beneficial for the company, whose products are promoted, and for those who contribute to this promotion.

In general, this type of cooperation is beneficial for both parties: with the growth of the Internet, it becomes more and more relevant, because to produce a product is only half of the battle, the essential thing is to be able to sell!

Affiliate Marketing: How to Start and How to Succeed

Unlike many other types of businesses outside the Internet, to start using affiliate marketing, you do not need to have some significant start-up capital. One of the reasons many people fail to succeed in this type of business is that they do not want to follow any proven method and try to do everything at once. If you want to achieve high results in affiliate marketing, you must find and choose the process that is tested and practiced by someone. In this article, we have prepared some tips and recommendations that will help you.

- **Success requires patience**

At first, you must understand that this kind of business will not bring you millions in one night. Yes, and for that, you must have the basic knowledge that we will convey to you in this article. If you are ready for it, then dare, but it is essential to understand that it takes time to master this knowledge in practice. It took us more than a year from the beginning of the site before the first revenue from affiliate sales occurred.

- **Your audience is more important than the percentage of sales.**

Everyone wants to get a high income immediately, but you should not forget that the customers you attract to buy affiliate products can potentially become your customers. Your visitors are the source of vitality for your business, so do not pay attention only to a high percentage of sales. However, this idea is more understandable for those who will provide services or sell their products without being limited to affiliates.

- **You need a website**

Even if you create a quality group on Facebook or Instagram with a well organized structure, you will not have total control over your company, your content can be deleted at any time for various reasons, so you need to create your own own website, which you will manage yourself, and create your customer base on this site.

- **Selection of a market segment**

Choosing a field of activity in which you want to work is not an easy task, chances are you choose a field that can not bring you a penny, and as a result, you're wasting time and effort, you do not want that. Are people looking for content related to this area? Can I somehow solve the problems of my potential customers? How many other serious companies can be found in Google for your research? Can you compete with them and make money? Do I understand how this area can become the best?

This last point is very important: it is hardly worth starting your own business without the desire to succeed, that is, to become the best. Success is achieved by those who set a goal, leadership, and continually reflect on how to do it.

- **Study well and love your business.**

We are convinced that you must not only know what you are saying, but also love it with all your soul ... Again, most successful people become so precisely because they live their own business ... If you do not Do not wake up everyday, thinking about the exciting work you do and do not like what you do, you are unlikely to achieve serious results. If you recognize yourself in this field, we advise you to seriously rethink and, perhaps, to change the subject to a topic more interesting for you, because even if you succeed in this area, you will get tired sooner or later. That's why, when choosing a topic for a site, you should consider both its in-depth research and your passion for it.

Affiliate marketing: What to sell?

If you have already decided on the scope of the activities you want to do, it's time to decide what to promote and sell. This is a fundamental question because not everything has an immediate meaning in the sale. Here are some questions you need to answer and tips that you must listen to to understand what types of products and partner services you should promote.

- The best way to sell a product is to use it yourself, are you ready to buy it yourself before you start selling it?
- Does the advertised product match your content?

When advertising for other people's products and businesses, do not forget your reputation:

- Ask yourself if this product is of high quality and can satisfy the customer's needs.
- Does the seller / manufacturer of the product you are promoting provide after-sales services?
- Does the seller's page seek to attract visitors and encourage them to buy goods?

Where to find an affiliate Products?

This is perhaps the most tedious, but the essential part of the whole process. Both individual companies offer affiliate programs and special networks to find such programs. We will start with the last one. Affiliate networks are sites that control each seller's affiliate programs and on these sites you can find hundreds of vendors who want to find partners to participate in their programs. Most of them work on the principle of "pay per sale" or "pay per lead". If you see that someone's product is sold on a website, try contacting the seller directly. It is more cost-effective and convenient to work this way, but you should trust only reliable and authorized sellers.

You can also explore the sites of your competitors and find affiliate programs for the products they sell. AdSense banners operate on the proven principle of contextual advertising: they know what ads and content are most successful, why not use their example: display an AdSense unit on your blog and see what type of ads appear on your pages. Once you have determined which pages are generating more revenue, you can delete that block on those pages.

1. Where to place affiliate links and banners?

The banner will only give real results if it is placed inside the container. That's exactly what Google AdSense recommends. Google prefers to place such ads that are really related to the content so that they blend in with the text and are an integral part of your site. If a visitor spends time reading it and is very interested in the information provided, it would be logical to tell them about the product that will interest them, which certainly increases their chances of buying it.

2. Only use quality content.

Each article you write carefully gives you the opportunity to make a profit, so take it seriously: the text should not only be unique, it must attract the customer with valuable information and make him want to buy goods.

3. Achieve targeted traffic

To find out if your content and affiliate links bring results, you need to attract a certain circle of visitors to your site.

Here are some quick tips to attract the target audience to your site:

- Write guest articles on third-party sites where you can find potential customers
- Share your content on social networks
- Create a free PDF file (for example, a short report) that leads to your content
- Work with subscribers by email , informing them of new articles on the site

4. Use a reliable and fast web host

If you want to use affiliate marketing on your website successfully, you should not use free hosting or Blogger type platforms. When choosing the web host, you must evaluate it with regard to businesses. Will your site receive quality services without interruption? Cheap accommodation can guarantee this. We have already talked about the disadvantages of free hosting in a clearer way. Therefore, we recommend that you do not waste time on such a decision and choose a truly worthy hosting company.

Remember, you do not have to change your business model until you feel sufficiently experienced in using a particular work method. If you follow this opinion, you will succeed. If your visitors are not very concerned about the number of affiliate links being placed on your site then your main task is that you should help them find a product, providing a convenient opportunity to buy it by setting the required number of links. affiliation to the right places. This will allow you to succeed affiliate marketing.

STEPS TO ATTRACT AFFILIATES TO YOUR PRODUCTS

Discover steps to attract Affiliates to your product. Your product has finally been created and is ready to be sold? This is the time to disclose it and finding good affiliates for your online course is one way to grow your sales quickly. But if achieving your product disclosure with the help of good affiliates is still a problem for you, this publication teaches how to attract real business partners in 10 steps and how to get the attention of affiliates who can bring your product at the next level. But, before showing how to attract affiliates we need to make clear what are the 3 possible forms of affiliate system setup within Hotmart.

- **Closed Affiliate Program**

In this mode the producer chooses not to use the Hotmart affiliate program. This is an option that, while valid, is not recommended for those who want to quickly increase sales of their product.

- **Only previously approved affiliates will be able to promote the product**

You take the option in favor of the affiliate program, so you can decide exactly who can disclose the product based on your own requirements. This is the ideal option for producers who want to find people willing to promote and generate sales, but want to know exactly who will promote its products.

- **All affiliates will be able to promote the product**

Leaving affiliation open to any affiliate is an opportunity to conquer many promoters quickly. However, it is important to explain that in this case, the producer must be attentive to the way your product is disclosed and how the interaction among your affiliates happens. Once you have set up your affiliate system you just have to convince affiliates to promote your product / To accompany you in this direction, i have prepared 10 steps you need to follow to promote your product:

1 - Take care of the profile picture of your product on Hotmart

In most cases, the affiliate has the first contact with your product on Hotmart. Through many products, your product struggles to attract attention with thousands of others. So that's why inserting an attractive image is the first thing you need to do.

The chosen photo must be in JPG, PNG or GIF format and have a maximum size of 2 M bytes. Using your producer's picture or your company logo together with something that characterizes your product is a great option. Producers who are more attentive to the value of a good affiliate use this space to highlight certain benefits for affiliates, such as commission, promotions and even prizes for those who achieve good results.

2 - Write on-the-fly Information for Affiliates exactly what you expect

The description space of your product is where the affiliate will understand what your product is. There is an information space here, and unfortunately many producers forget to insert a good text: clear and persuasive. This space was created to explain to you what the needs are to disclose your product and how the affiliate can get in touch with you. Another important point of this description is to highlight what are the benefits of promoting your product. That is to say here is the place to show just how attractive your affiliate is.

3 - Use groups and forums to attract affiliates for your business

To attract good affiliates, it is not enough to put the product on the market, because, as to find good suppliers, partners and partners, it takes effort, it is indeed necessary to go in search of the best affiliates.

The simplest channels to contact potential affiliates to disclose your product is by interacting in groups on Facebook about the topic or on discussion forums. On these spaces, it is possible to exchange ideas with affiliates who, like you, are interested in increasing their sales. Affiliates are part of your business and they need to be treated as partners to build a lasting relationship.

4- Transform people who have a relationship with your market niche into affiliates

The affiliate market is still unknown by many people, even those with sites and pages with a large audience. Inviting them to start working with Hotmart by starting with your product is one way to get qualified affiliates to learn the rules of the game.

For example, if you have a lesson on how to play the guitar and you know a youtubeuse with a large audience that makes hits hits, you can invite him to make a small disclosure of your product in exchange for commissions. This is one of the steps to conquer more affiliates demanding the producer the most patience.

5- Participate in events in the field

In addition to exploring forums and communities on the Internet, you can start attending events near you. Good networking is very often what you need to start your partnership with the right affiliate for your audience.

6- Create exclusive materials for your affiliates

Affiliates need content to do a good job on your product. Make banners, put pictures for editing at their disposal, inform exactly who the target audience is, in short make your affiliate's job easier.

A great way to do this is to create different sales pages, tailored to the diverse needs of the affiliate. For example, an affiliate who works with e-mail disclosure needs a page with less detail than a user who uses Facebook ads as their primary source of traffic.

7- Offer a fair commission

Each product has an average selling cost for the affiliate. There are cases where this cost is low and the affiliate quickly recovers the cost of the sale with the profit he receives through the commission. While in other cases, mainly when the product is new, this cost is unknown and must be tested.

For this reason, the commission you offer must cover the costs of selling and still provide a profit margin to the promoter. So if you offer a very low commission, it is likely that affiliates will run away from your product. Look at the products on Hotmart which is the percentage of the commission compared to the prices charged by the competition. This will help you understand the values that the market already practices, even if your product is new.

8- Give access to Hotmart tools

Hotmart has several tools that help the affiliate to disclose your product. However, for them to enjoy everything we create, you need to enable certain features. One of the favourite tools of affiliates who also produce content is Automatic Bonus Delivery. With this system, it is possible to deliver files or sites together with the product that is disclosed and Hotmart is responsible for sending this content automatically to your buyer. That is to say, the affiliate does not need to worry about the delivery of this bonus but can use it as a marketing argument to encourage his public to spend on the purchase.

Another option that is fundamental for your affiliates is the use of Hotleads on your e-mail capture pages. It is through this tool that the lead generated by an affiliate is marked and, if he buys your product, Hotmart also identifies by e-mail the sales manager. Both need to be empowered by you and are very simple to configure, okay?

9- Keep a constant conversation with your affiliates

As we mentioned at the beginning of this post, understanding that the affiliate is a business partner is the best way for you to manage to extract the best of his work. Large producers usually have on their team the role of Affiliate Manager, a professional who can answer many requests from affiliates and, most importantly, direct them on how to do a good job.

But, even if you do not have a team, doing this role of attention to your business partners is vital to your growth. Listening to them and thinking about ways to make them more productive is your job as a producer. Make recurring meetings via Skype with the best and try to help those who are not doing well, but who show interest and potential. Never forget: they are with you in your business.

10- Be your own affiliate

Nothing better to know what your affiliate wants and needs than being your own promoter. Selling your own product, in addition to being fundamental to the independence of your business, is important for you to speak at the same level as your affiliates.

AMAZON ASSOCIATES: HOW TO CHPOSE AND PROMOTE THE MOST PROFITABLE PRODUCTS

How to choose and promote the most profitable products

This guide contains practical tips for promoting the most profitable and best-suited products for your site or blog in order to boost your activities in the context of the Partners Club.

In the program :

- Why use Amazon AssociatesHow to identify and define your nicheTips for choosing profitable products to promote in your niche
- Why use Amazon Associates

Amazon is one of the largest and most popular markets in the world. The partner marketing program, the Partner Club, is the best choice for affiliate site owners. Beginners and veterans of affiliate marketing will probably be successful with the affiliate club. When you promote products for sale on Amazon, you earn commissions.

In addition, even when customers who come to Amazon after clicking on one of your links buy products other than the one you recommended, you still have a chance to earn a commission. Regular payments, easy-to-use tools, incredible benefits and increased conversion rates: The Partners Club is here to help you increase your income.

The benefits of the Amazon Partner Club

Finding the Right Products and the Right Niche: The Biggest Challenge for Affiliate Marketers

To succeed with the Partner Club, you must make several important decisions. To begin, you must choose the right products to promote. Millions of items are selling on Amazon; it is therefore impossible to put them all forward.

To increase your Partner Club revenue, you must promote the products that are most in tune with your site, your visitors and your subscribers. This article explains how to choose the products to promote on your site or blog.

How to identify and define your niche

Any Partner Club member must decide if he or she should create a site on a topic that is passionate about him or a topic that involves high commissions. There is no ready answer. However, you should choose a niche that will continue to interest you. For example, if you like gadgets, a blog about the latest news, updates, reviews and tutorials about it could be perfect for you, because you'll have no trouble writing articles or making videos.

Tips for choosing profitable products to promote in your niche

To earn commissions using your blog or Partner Club website, you must carefully select the products you are promoting. Here are some tips to help you find the most profitable products:

1. The best sales in your niche

When you have chosen your topic, research the most profitable products sold on Amazon. Look for products that are relevant, of good quality, profitable and that sell well. Amazon offers all kinds of tools to help you. First, go to Amazon and find the product category that fits your niche. For example, if your site is dedicated to women's skincare products, go to Amazon.com, then click on Our categories, then Beauty and Fragrances. Use filters to find the products that best fit your niche in this category.

You can sort the search results using the "Average Customer Feedback" setting to find the top rated products. You can also use the Amazon best seller page to identify which products sell best in each category. Promoting products mentioned on the best sellers page encourages visitors to go to the act of purchase, which earns you commissions. There are also great ways to rank the products you recommend on your blog and present your favourite lists .

2. High value products

As part of the Partner Club, you earn a percentage on all sales made; it's your commission. When you promote more expensive products, there is a good chance that your commissions will increase.

For example, if you earn 10% commission by promoting a product, you can earn $20 by selling a $200 product. However, when you put forward a product worth 2€, you must encourage 100 of your visitors to buy it to earn the same commission of 20€.

This does not mean that it is useless to promote cheaper products. You can earn good commissions by promoting cheap products, but for that you have to sell a lot. Remember that the Amazon cookie that returns your visitors to the Amazon site remains active for 24 hours. You will earn commissions on all products purchased during this period. Learn how to unlock the potential of your site

3. Timeless products

Some products make the buzz before disappearing. On the other hand, others are timeless and sell for years, surviving all modes. It can be helpful to identify some timeless products in your niche and publish tickets promoting them. These notes could continue to earn commissions over time.

4. Eligible Premium Products

The ease of purchase and shipping plays a vital role in the purchase decision. Amazon has revolutionized online shopping by making it easy. Best of all, Amazon Prime users enjoy several benefits, such as same-day delivery, priority access to certain offers, and more.

One of the biggest benefits of the Prime program is free shipping for all eligible products. When looking for products to promote, it may be helpful to prioritize Prime products; Premium subscribers will be tempted to reap the benefits and purchase.

5. Preferred products

To find the most popular products, check out their ratings. Products with a large number of ratings (more than 50) are considered good products that are probably selling well.

Be sure to check the date of the evaluations. This could give you an idea of how often a product is sold to determine if it has good sales potential, or if it is out of date.

6. Find the products put forward by the competition

Visit the affiliate sites of your competitors to get an idea of the products they promote. For example, say you own a blog about photography. You would do well to visit the affiliate sites devoted to this art to see their content and the recommended products. This could give you product ideas for your site.

7. Focus on targeted traffic

The majority of your Amazon affiliate site traffic is likely to come from users looking for products / reviews / descriptions. The keywords used can be:

- Key phrases: for example, mobile phones under € 300 unlocked
- Generic keywords: buy latest cell phones

Traffic resulting from these keywords is targeted because the user makes a purchase. These users are looking for product information to make an informed decision. When writing tickets, be sure to focus on key phrases, as generic keywords are widely used; so it is difficult to get a good ranking. By focusing on key phrases, you are more likely to attract targeted traffic, and therefore more likely to make a purchase.

For example, instead of writing an article about fitness equipment, you could create several tickets targeting specific groups: fitness equipment for those who suffer from chronic pain, fitness equipment for those who are preparing for run a marathon, etc.

8. Look for key phrases to incorporate into your content

This will give you an idea of all the other keywords that you can include in your content. If you have just joined the Partner Club, it can be very difficult to get a good ranking for keywords as generic as "Best Camera". On the other hand, by creating key phrase posts like "Best Camera to Record Videos," "Best Camera for YouTube Videos," you can attract targeted traffic and promote specialized products.

9. Products that appeal to your target audience

Say you have a blog about cooking recipes; promoting laptops and electronics will not be of interest to your target audience. Before choosing a product to put forward on your site, make sure that it appeals to your audience.

For this, ask directly to your visitors the kind of tickets they would like to read on your blog. This way, you can promote products that match the preferences of your target audience.

10. Use Google Trends

Google Trends is a great tool for identifying trendy products. This tool also helps you track the search volume of keywords. This could give you a good idea of the popularity of a particular product and help you determine if it can lead to good sales.

Finding the right products is the key to success

As a member of the Amazon Partner Club, you have access to millions of products on Amazon. However, your success and your income depend on the products you put forward. Use the tips in this article for your Amazon affiliate site or blog, and choose the products that are most likely to interest your target audience. This is how you will increase your sales, and therefore your commissions.

ESSENTIAL TIPS FOR BLOGGERS WHO START AFFILIATE MARKETING

It is undeniable that affiliate marketing is an important source of income. It is also for people who are looking for serious money or who want to support themselves through this profession.

I. Affiliate marketing can make you earn money seriously

Without a doubt, it is an attractive source of money. But, rolling this money train is not as easy as it seems. There must be careful planning and a lot of execution behind these affiliate conversions. Let's review 5 things that bloggers should follow if they want to embark on affiliate marketing:

II. Connect with the public

Who will buy the products you will try to sell? The readers of the blog or the public. But before buying something, they must trust you. Trust is not developed in a day. It takes a lot of work and creativity to produce pivotal articles that appeal to the target audience. Thus, key elements like regularity, quality of content and engagement are prerequisites for establishing good contact with your audience.

III. Shrink your sphere

I'm not telling you to limit your thinking, but more specifically the topics you are writing about. If you write about electronics once and then move on to the lifestyle, it will be difficult for you to have a very targeted audience on your blog. This will directly affect product sales. If you try to promote a shampoo and half of the readership is not interested in shampoo but in electronics, you have already halved your conversion rate. Therefore, niche blogging is better than general blogging!

IV. Learn from others

Affiliate marketing is an art. You have to master the art of convincing to make the sale. This art may not be inherent in your personality, but it can be learned by others. The simple mantra is to read, read and learn more about affiliate marketing. Learn from the experiences of others.

WHY AFFILIATE MARKETING IS PROFITABLE

Many bloggers are not interested in affiliate marketing. Either they think it's too difficult, it's a waste of time, they will lose readers and the audience, that their readers will simply not be interested. In fact, most bloggers earn $ 500 or less per month through affiliate marketing . These include bloggers who receive 1,000,000 page views or more each month. These bloggers all have the same problem. They do not realize how much money they leave on the table and they have no idea how to approach affiliate marketing the right way.

This is something that often scares bloggers and social media influencers away from affiliate marketing. They are afraid of what their readers will say or think and they are afraid to pretend to be greedy salesmen. It's just not true. Few people complain about the affiliate products that are promoted on blogs. When done the right way, affiliate marketing can be a good source of income. Plus, you can do it without taking away your readers! If it's done the right way, your readers will enjoy seeing the products that interest you and they will have no problem making purchases through your affiliate links. Affiliate marketing is interesting for many reasons, as you will read below.

- **Affiliate marketing is a somewhat passive source of income.**

Affiliate marketing is profitable because you can write an article, a product comparison and this article and this comparative product can save you money years later with a minimum of work necessary to maintain it.

- **But it's not entirely passive.**

You will need to build a follow-up, publish content consistently, build trust, and more. You can get income from an affiliate link or blog post for a long period of time, with little work needed to maintain it.

- **There is less work than creating your own product with affiliate marketing.**

Affiliate marketing is not easy, but there are things you do not have to worry about when you compare affiliate marketing versus creating your own product.

You do not need to ship anything, create the product, manage cancellations, manage customer service and more. Yes, you will have to build your audience and gain the trust of your readers, but it can be a great way to increase your income, especially if you already have followers.

- **Affiliate marketing is inexpensive.**

The low cost of affiliate marketing is another reason why it is a great way to increase your income. You do not need to create products or spend time building a product.

You do not even need a website because you can start promoting affiliate products on social media accounts such as Facebook, Twitter and Instagram. If you decide to have a website, it can also be relatively affordable, because launching a website does not cost much today.

- **You can be paid to promote products you believe in.**

There are bound to be a lot of products that you like and appreciate. So, why not get paid to talk to others? Plus, if you really like a product, it will be easy to promote. You will already know everything about the product and you will have no problem to be enthusiastic about it. If the product has helped you, it will probably help other people too and people will appreciate your honest opinion.

There are many options for the products to promote. There are so many products, services and businesses to promote. There is something for every taste ! Here are some examples of products you could promote to your audience:

- Financial corporations
- Mobile phone applications
- Digital products, such as online courses, eBooks, etc.
- One of millions of articles on Amazon
- Travel
- Booking
- Websites
- Blog-related products, such as website design, website hosting, etc.
- Clothing
- Interior decoration
- Craft articles
- Outdoor equipment such as bicycles, tents, backpacks, etc.

However, do not believe that with affiliate marketing, you will enrich yourself quickly because this is not the case. You will need to build a loyal audience that trusts what you have to say, and it's not always easy. However, if you are able to build an audience that is interested in your editorial line then you may be able to earn money by promoting products that you like and believe in.

You can work from anywhere with affiliate marketing.

One of the best benefits of affiliate marketing is that you can do it from anywhere. As long as you have a loyal audience (even if it's only a few people), a laptop. Thanks to your blog and affiliate marketing, you will be able to travel full time. All you need is a good internet connection and good articles and products. It's really something great! Affiliate marketing is an easy concept to learn, but it can be very addictive to learn if you are new. Affiliate marketing is a method to try to make money by placing an affiliate link on your website, social media account, etc. and that people buy a product through your link.

An affiliate is a person or company who promotes a product or service offered by other companies. You become an affiliate when you promote an affiliate product. An example are Amazon book sales, where you link to a specific book on your website and try to get people to buy the book through your affiliate link. Amazon and other companies want quality affiliates to promote the products and services they sell.

If you get someone to sign up through your affiliate link, you are then rewarded by the company for promoting their product. This is called a conversion. A conversion is when a person performs a specific action defined by the affiliate program. It can be someone who enters their email address on a company's website, makes a purchase, completes a form, or any other action through your affiliate link.

You can share an affiliate link with your audience in different ways, such as:

- By adding an affiliate link to your blog (you can do this by inserting a link into a blog post, page, email, etc.
- Promotion on social media
- Share the information in a podcast or webinar.   And many other methods!

Why would a company be interested in affiliate marketing?

Companies are becoming more interested in affiliate marketing because it can be a great way to promote their products. And they only have to pay a commission if there is a conversion. Many companies like this option, because they often spend a lot of money on advertising but do not get quality leads. With affiliate marketing, the company pays only if a sale is made or if it receives a lead, a contact.

Affiliate marketing is great for online influencers.

For online influencers, affiliate marketing can be a great way to make money by simply reviewing or mentioning a product you already enjoy and love. In return, your contribution influences others to buy the product. Affiliate revenue can be important because you can create an article that continues to earn you money years later.

When it comes to affiliate marketing, there are just a few easy steps to get you started:

- Find a product or affiliate service to promote a product or service relevant to your brand
- Sign up and get approval for the product affiliate program
- Insert your affiliate link on your website or social media accounts
- Refer people to your affiliate link and do conversions
- Receive commissions for conversions you make

How affiliate links work

The way affiliate links works is that when someone clicks on the referral link that you have received from an affiliate program (this will be a specific URL just for you or a code that tracks the traffic that you send to the company), you receive commissions when they complete a certain action. Then you receive your commission payment either by check, PayPal, or any other method that you and the affiliate program agree on.

Your referrals are tracked through a referral link given to you by an affiliate program. This reference link contains a code in the URL that follows the origin of the reference. When someone clicks on your affiliate link, a "cookie" is stored on the computer, tablet or mobile of the user to track purchases via your affiliate link. In a cookie, information such as your affiliate ID, the IP address of the customer, the date he clicked on your affiliate link, and so on. are all stored. This then allows affiliate programs to track the origin of clicks and conversions.

An affiliate click or conversion can also be tracked through a special coupon code that can be given to you by the affiliate program. For example, "FOUINETEAU25%

REM" can be an affiliate coupon code that allows you to receive a commission. In this way, the affiliate program can know and trace where the user comes from.

What is considered a conversion?

The action that determines whether a conversion has occurred, as mentioned above, depends on the specific affiliate program, but usually it's either when someone buys something through your link, when he signs up for a account, or give his e-mail address to the company. Yes, it means that a purchase does not always have to take place! Let me repeat the above, sometimes a person just needs to create an account or sign up for a mailing list so you can earn a commission. It all depends on the specific affiliate program, but about half of the affiliate products that are promoted just require the person to create an account.

How to be paid with affiliate marketing?

There are three main ways to get paid via affiliate marketing. These include:

- **Percentage of sale amount**

According to this method, if someone buys something through your link, you will receive a percentage of the sale amount. So if the product is 100 € and you receive 25% for each sale, you will receive 25 €. The percentages can vary considerably, from 1% to 50% and more.

- **Fixed base**

When you are paid on a fixed basis, you will earn income every time someone buys something through your link. However, you will be paid the same amount regardless of the amount spent.

- **By contact called lead**

For this, you will be paid a certain amount for each prospect that you send to the company. A lead can be thought of as someone who gives the company his email address, registering to create an account, etc. If you are able to direct a large amount of traffic to the business, paying by lead or prospect can be a great way to earn money through affiliate marketing. However, the pay per lead payment is not as high as the other two methods.

How long is an affiliate code followed?

The different affiliate programs have different deadlines depending on when the customer has completed the action. For some affiliate programs, you may receive commissions for years after the user has clicked on your affiliate link (this is commonly called life cookies), for others you may receive a commission on each product that the person buys. For other programs, you are only paid up to 30 days after clicking on your affiliate link, and so on.

The time varies depending on the affiliate program.

Longer times are better because a person often does not buy a product or become a lead right away. They can think about the purchase or they can close the Internet window, but you still want to receive a commission if they register later. This gives the customer more time to think about the purchase, which gives you a better chance of winning a conversion.

HOW TO FIND AFFILIATE PRODUCTS

If you like a product, there is probably an affiliate program. Some companies even have their own affiliate systems just for their specific products. And, there are also affiliate programs with hundreds, and sometimes thousands, of products listed in their network (we call them "affiliate networks").

There are many ways to find affiliate programs. These include:

- Search online
- Affiliate Networks
- Directly through the company
- Ask businesses and friends

Search online

If there is a specific product that you would like to promote, we recommend doing a quick Google search to see if the company has an affiliate program. You can do this simply by typing "Company or Product Name + Affiliate Program".

This search will allow you to see exactly where their affiliate program is, so you can apply and be accepted as quickly as possible. For example: To see if Amazon has an affiliate program, type "Amazon Affiliate Program." As you can see in the picture below, this is the very first thing that appears.

Affiliate Networks

Affiliate networks are companies that list a large number of companies and products. This is a way for you to apply for an affiliate network while being introduced to hundreds or even thousands of different affiliate products.

To be a member of an affiliate network, you usually only have to complete an online application. The app asks questions about your website, social media accounts, and intentions that motivate you to join the affiliate network.

Affiliate networks are interesting because:

- You only have to make one application for the program, while receiving access to many different affiliate products
- It's easier to track your payments from an affiliate network if you use more than one of their affiliate products

Affiliate networks ensure that individual businesses within their program follow certain rules (such as ensuring that companies are able to pay you commissions).

Direct Affiliate Programs

Many companies publish their affiliate programs directly on their website. Some companies are not part of an affiliate network and run their own affiliate programs. We are seeing an increase in the number of companies doing this and more and more companies are running their own affiliate programs. If there is a specific company that interests you, go to the company's website and look for the word "affiliate" or "reference" at the bottom of their home page.

Ask the company or friends who are affiliated

There is a probability that a company's affiliate program is a bit difficult to find. If so, she may not have an affiliate program or be aware of how difficult it is to find their program. If you can not find their affiliate program, we recommend contacting them directly and asking them, "Do you have an affiliate program? Or, if you know someone who is already an affiliate of the company, you can see if he will introduce you to their affiliate manager.

HOW TO CHOOSE THE RIGHT AFFILIATE PROGRAM TO PROMOTE

As you just read, there are many ways to find affiliate products. It is also possible for a product to be in more than one affiliate program. If you find a product in several programs, you should evaluate the benefits of each program to determine which one is best for you. You will evaluate:

- **The commission rate**

This can vary from one affiliate program to another! Keep in mind that the commission rate is not the most important thing. Often, a product with a low commission rate can earn you more money than a product with a higher commission rate. You should always promote the products and services that you believe in first, then think about the commission.

- **Conversion specifications**

Sometimes a conversion may be based on the percentage of the sale amount, on a fixed basis, or per prospect, which is discussed in more detail above in the section on the operation of affiliate links. These specifics may vary from one affiliate program to another, so you will want to compare to see which one is best for the type of product you want to promote.

- **The duration of cookies**

When promoting a product, the duration of cookies is important. Not all customers will buy an item after clicking on it and some may even wait months. The longer the length of cookies, the better.

- **Management of the affiliate program**

Some affiliate program managers are nice while others are not. An excellent partnership with your affiliate manager can lead to better commission rates, faster sales notice, search help, coupon codes for your audience, and more.

- **Conviviality**

Some affiliate programs are easier to use and easier for your readers than others. Usability includes things such as landing pages just designated for your. Would you buy personally or would you sign up for a specific affiliation offer if you were a member of your audience? If the answer is no, then move on!

In conclusion, there are many ways to find affiliate programs for the products you want to promote. After finding an affiliate program that interests you, you will want to apply or see what needs to be done for you to be accepted. Once you are accepted, you can then find your affiliate link in the specific program.

WHY YOU SHOULD USE SOCIAL MEDIA

Many freelancers rarely use social media to find customers and think that the best advertising is word-of-mouth. Others have made the effort to create a showcase site to have a reference tool to submit and are registered on many social media. Very often, the results are not up to their expectations. Let's see why?

What is social media exactly?

To find out whether or not social media can be of interest to your business, it's worth revisiting its definition. In "social media" there are two words:

- Media: means of communication and dissemination of information.
- Social: Who says "social" says exchange of tastes, points of view.

As you know, a user no longer consults the content of websites without being able to act or react. With Web 2.0, the user becomes active, can express himself, give his opinion, leave a comment. Through social media, the Internet has become more interactive and participatory. The user is positioned at the heart of the system and becomes a real actor by sharing photos, videos or commenting on the content published by others.

The real advantage of a social media

So we can easily conclude that the real benefit of social media for a business is being close to and interacting with their customers. So before thinking of improving its e-reputation, visibility, etc., thanks to social media, we must instead focus first on the expectations of users based on the media used. Each social media has its particularity, its utility and aims at a type of people. For example, if you are targeting individuals, LinkedIn will not help you to achieve your goal, whatever it may be.

They revolutionized the way we use the web. Your presence on social media will be of real benefit to your business if you succeed in creating a strong social connection between you and the internet users, between you and a specific target .

Social media for what use?

Often, when we talk about social media, we think of classic social networks like Facebook. Social networks are just one category of social media. For example, blogs and forums are social media without being social networks in their own right.

In fact, social media that encompasses all social platforms in the broad sense can be grouped into categories according to their usefulness. It is found for all tastes and for all uses. Here are the most well known by type of social media:

- **Consumer Social Network: Facebook**

Facebook is a very popular social network that allows everyone to stay in touch with family, friends and also with their professional sphere. Facebook allows targeted advertising (Facebook ads) and access to applications aimed at selling products online. Although Facebook is a BtoC-oriented social network, this medium is also suitable for businesses:

i. Capable of producing shareable content (photos, videos).
ii. Having an advertising budget to boost their content, targeting their audience.

- **Professional social media: LinkedIn, Viadeo**

LinkedIn is the most popular professional social network, leader in the international market. It allows any business to get their business page, share content, prospect and get in touch with prospects or customers. It also allows a company to recruit candidates for a job offer.

LinkedIn offers a diverse advertising program (banners, targeted emails, sponsored posts) that is extremely expensive. Moreover, on LinkedIn, the time of use is much less important than on Facebook. Like LinkedIn, Viadeo (French social network) makes it possible to find customers, partners, employees ... and thus facilitates dialogue between professionals.

- **Micro-blogging social network: Twitter**

Twitter is social media that allows you to watch and share information in real time. The communication is done through short messages (280 characters): the Tweets.

Twitter is above all a social media adapted to companies

I. BtoC able to produce virality with good content;
II. BtoB wishing to interact with the influencers of their market.

- **Blogging social media: WordPress, Blogger, Tumblr**

These publishing platforms are used to publish and share all types of content (articles, videos, audios). Users can leave comments for each publication. The most used social media for blogging is WordPress, supported by a very large community. WordPress is a very flexible CMS that adapts to our needs and desires. I wholeheartedly recommend it to you. That said, if you have little computer knowledge, it is much better to go through a provider for its creation.

- **Video media: YouTube, Vimeo, Dailymotion**

This type of media will allow you to broadcast and share videos to your audience. Users can view, share and leave comments. YouTube is the most important social media for video sharing.

YouTube is especially suitable for companies that can produce:

I. Videos that create emotion and also based on storytelling techniques.
II. Tutorials offering a solution to the problems of their audience.

- **Social networks of visuals: Pinterest, Flickr, Instagram, Prisma**

This type of media allows the management and sharing of photos on the Internet. For example, with Pinterest, you can share your interests through photographs found on the Internet. Any company has the opportunity to present visuals (photos, computer graphics, etc.) to enhance its expertise on these social media. Nevertheless, it should be noted that some areas of activity are much more attractive than others: fashion, cuisine, design, luxury, etc.

- **Slideshow Media: Slideshare**

SlideShare is a social media hosting and sharing slide presentations. You can produce content in the form of a slide show and expand your audience. Slideshare is a medium suited to any company wishing to demonstrate its expertise and know-how by enhancing their PowerPoint presentations. Bloggers can also use this media to enrich their articles.

- **Q & A: Yahoo Answers, Quora, Ask.fm**

These social networks allow any user to ask questions and answer questions from other users. So it is a very good way to learn about the questions asked by your market niche. And so, quickly get article topics to write.

- **Wikis media: Wikipedia**

A wiki is a collaborative social media that allows any visitor to edit or add content. The best known is Wikipedia, a participatory encyclopedia on the Web. The content of Wikipedia is for the most part a very good resource for bloggers. They have the opportunity to use Wikipedia to present additional information to their publications.

- **Content Sharing Media: Scoop-it**

Scoop.it allows everyone to create an online newspaper on a specific topic and distribute it to their network to build their professional brand. Scoop.it is considered by many to be the most effective and easiest content curation platform. In addition to your corporate blog, this social media can allow you to share and classify many sources of information to create an expert image on a specific topic.

- **Collaborative media: Trello, Slack**

With this type of collaborative communication platform, each company can create a private group, invite its employees or partners to share content and interact with all registered members. Trello is a very good tool for organizing your personal or team work. I strongly advise you to use it. Very easy to use, intuitive interface, this tool will allow you to boost your productivity!

- **Music Media: Soundcloud, Spotify, Deezer, MySpace**

These online audio distribution platforms offer musicians the means to promote and distribute their musical projects. Although these platforms are initially positioned on music, they can also be used to host and publish your podcasts (downloadable online audio file), safely.

Other applications

- **Mobile Apps**: Snapchat, PathMobile.
- **Messaging apps:** Facebook messenger, Whatsapp, Wechat, Viber, Line.

Why use social media?

Many trainers and freelancers have not taken the digital turn and continue to prospect their customers with traditional tools (phone, email).

This type of prospecting requires a lot of work and ultimately brings few results for two reasons:

- Today's consumers will search for information on Google and social media themselves before making a purchase decision. That's why it's very difficult to get an appointment with a prospect who does not know you. The success of a company depends not only on the quality of its services, but also on its network and its visibility. Consumers trust companies that are recognized on the web.
- It's easy to understand the importance of making your business visible on the channels your potential customers use. The visibility and reputation of your company on the Internet will therefore have a direct impact on your turnover.

Being present on social networks is not a fashion, but a necessity. Above all, it should be noted that the use of social media affects the overall communication of your company. The presence of your company on a social media is very time-consuming and the expected results will cover the duration. The time factor is therefore an important criterion to consider before establishing its strategy on social media.

The second important thing to understand is that your presence on a social network such as Facebook will not allow you to differentiate yourself effectively from the competition or at least to establish a real independent social communication. For example, since January 11, 2018, the significant modification of the Facebook algorithm now requires companies to invest in Facebook ads to increase the organic reach of their publications (and reach the majority of their fans). In other words, a company that uses Facebook must accept this dependency and any future rule changes.

At the moment, it is therefore essential for a company to have its blog (and not a simple showcase site) to be able to:

- Have your hands on your own publishing platform
- Share his vision, his ideas

- Produce high value-added content that can be shared
- Interact with their audience and establish a concrete relationship with their subscribers.

The blog, a necessity. The blog is therefore the anchor of your strategy on social media, the "independent center" of your social communication. The more relevant your content is to your visitors, the more it will be relayed by itself on social networks such as Facebook and Twitter. So your blog will allow you to touch the social circles of people who have shared your content. Of course, this virality can not take place without a real content strategy, without an editorial line close to the expectations of your readers. The mistake is to use only social media as an additional means of communication to make sales. Internet users are present on social networks for entertainment, find specific information, share their opinion and not to hear a commercial speech.

The marketing of social networks is primarily a marketing of listening.

You must of course share your knowledge, give useful information, but it is also important to know how to listen to your interlocutors. Social networks are places of exchange and we must not forget it. By remaining in a logic of sharing and conversation, you will increase your sympathy capital. Indirectly, the sales will follow in a second time thanks to your community animation.

1. Listen to your interlocutors

By listening to your interlocutors, social networks will bring you:

- Targeted contacts
- Increase in the number of relationships
- Creating a community around your brand
- Improving your e-reputation

2. A real plus in terms of natural referencing
- Creating backlinks (incoming links) to your blog
- Improved positioning on search engines
- Increase your blog traffic

The community must be at the center of your social media strategy. The more engaged your community is, the more likely you are to convert your audience into customers. Otherwise, by rushing to be present on many social media without having the time to animate them, having as a priority objective to sell, for example your online training, you may be very disappointed by your results.

In conclusion, having a blog and being present on social media (according to your objectives) to establish proximity with your customers is essential. If you do not use these communication channels in your strategy, you will lose the opportunity to acquire and retain many customers. Worse still, you are offering your competitors a considerable advantage.

WHICH SOCIAL NETWORK TO CHOOSE TO ADVERTISE YOUR BUSINESS?

Choosing a social network to make yourself known is not so simple. As we have seen, including social media in its communication plan is essential. However, to get all the benefits, it is important to choose them according to their specificities and according to your objectives.

Let's see which social network to choose for your affiliate marketing activity?

Social networks coupled with your blog are an integral part of your digital strategy. To be well known on social networks lies in choosing a good strategy.

Mistakes to avoid to become well known on social networks

To make oneself known on social networks and to create a community around one's brand requires a lot of time and method. I noticed that some affiliate marketer undermine their credibility on social networks, because they do not take the time to think and ultimately do not use any strategy. So before getting into the thick of it, it seems important to warn you about the various mistakes you could make:

- Do not set a concrete goal before choosing and embarking on a social network
- Spread out on many social networks and not take advantage of the potential of the social network most relevant to his business
- Do not take the time to fully understand the operation and rules of each social network
- Choose to be present on a social network because its competitor has chosen it
- Do not respond to comments and messages
- Publish irrelevant content for your target
- Use jargon or vocabulary that is not suitable for your audience
- Publish promotional content too frequently
- Have an irregular publication frequency

Each social network will be able if it is well used to bring you traffic to your website & blog. Nevertheless, before choosing a social network over another, it is necessary to determine with precision:

- Your target
- Your goals
- Your content strategy
- Your choices according to your resources

Key points to become well known on social networks

1. Determine your target

This is the first question to ask yourself: "Who are your products and services for? " Whether for your marketing in general or on social networks, we do not talk to everyone . As long as you do not have a clear idea of your target, it will be difficult for you to direct your communication effectively.

This study goes far beyond: my clients are individuals, businesses, young people, retirees ... If you have not yet identified your ideal customers and analysed their needs and expectations, I recommend, once again , to follow this free methodology: "The marketing strategy of trainer 2.0".

2. Determine your goals before choosing a social network

The first goal that comes to mind for any entrepreneur is to find customers through social networks. Yes, but still? Social networks are not tools dedicated to sales. Everyone has their own operating rules and will benefit you according to well-defined objectives.

Social networks can achieve 5 objectives overall:

- Develop a community around your values and gain notoriety
- Get a direct exchange with your community and your customers
- Develop your professional network, find BtoB clients and recruit new employees
- Improve the SEO of your website
- Attract influencers and prove your expertise

It is up to you to choose them according to the priority objective that you seek to achieve.

3. Develop your content strategy

Since social networks are communication tools with the objective of creating commitment in your community, it is important to define the messages you want to convey.

In other words, what is your editorial line?

- Identify the themes that you want to address
- Determine an editorial calendar and therefore the frequency of your publications
- Create relevant content or relay content from your watch
- Decide what kind of content you want to share: articles, videos, photos, computer graphics

Content is the foundation of a successful media social strategy. To develop your reputation and stand out from the competition:

- Focus your communication on information that is useful to your community and not promotional.
- Produce multimedia content and when possible use visuals adapted to each social network.
- Differentiate your editorial line for each social network.
- Study the communication of your competitors and analyse which contents generate the most commitments.

Share published articles from your blog on your social networks. Integrate social sharing buttons on each article so that your readers can share them to their audiences. Set up a newsletter and build a list of contacts. Holding a blog takes time and work just like running a social network . It is certain that the expected results will not be achieved overnight. But you will have a lot more success if you give rather than if you ask ...

4. Determine your choices according to your resources

Ideally, you think it would be nice to have your company on Facebook, LinkedIn, Instagram, YouTube, Twitter, etc. The question to ask yourself is "do you have the human resources to animate all these social networks? " Except if you are a team of several people, it is likely that you will not have time to communicate effectively on many social networks.

You must use them wisely according to their specificities and according to your objective. Initially if you are alone, for example if you are freelance or an independent trainer, I advise you:

- Focus your efforts on a single social network; and just relay your articles on others.
- Tell yourself that a social network without animation will serve you little and will waste your time rather than something else.

When you are alone in your business, you have to know how to make choices and not have eyes bigger than your stomach. Holding a blog already requires enough work and a day lasts only 24 hours.

Why choose this social network?

Facebook is the largest social network in the world.

In United state of america, there are about 30 million Facebook accounts with all age groups and population categories. A professional is first and foremost a person who, for the most part, has a Facebook profile. Even if Facebook is more BtoC oriented, it remains the essential social network for any company, big or small for:

- Develop a community around its values and gain notoriety
- Get a direct exchange with your community and customers

Facebook will allow your company to obtain high visibility among consumers, regardless of its status: students, employees, self-employed, retirees. In addition, in the vast majority of cases, you will get much more sharing on your articles with Facebook rather than with another social network (essential to boost its SEO!). This is a significant advantage to consider as well.

How to make yourself known on this social network?

Be aware that the use of your personal profile for a commercial activity is a prohibited practice and indicated in the terms of use of Facebook.

1 - The personal profile

As you most certainly know, a personal account allows a natural person to communicate and share with other people all kinds of content (articles, images, videos). Relationships are those of a natural person with other people. Any new relationship (becoming "friend") is necessarily linked to a consent (acceptance or not of the request).

Advantages

- Find new contacts directly
- Comment and share on another person's diary
- Send private messages to another person
- Intervene in Facebook groups

Disadvantages

- For personal and non-professional
- The number of friends is limited to 5000
- No statistics on publications to refine its strategy
- Can not advertise and hold contests

LThis support is the easiest way to set up to be followed and create a community around what you have to share.

2 - The professional page

This page will allow you to broadcast and promote content related to your business. The information is public, any natural person (so with a personal account) can follow your news and decide whether or not to become "Fan" (by clicking "I like"). The publications of your Pro page will then appear in the news feed of your "Fans". In theory … because the organic reach is in free fall (less than 5%). For example, if one of your Fans never interacted with your content, your posts will never be visible in his newsfeed …

Advantages

- Access to key indicators to measure the effectiveness of publications
- Possibility of being managed by several people
- Ability to advertise
- Possibility of organizing competitions

- No limit on the number of Fans

Disadvantages

- The organic reach of posts is very low
- Can not send a message to all his fans
- Can not directly prospect new contacts
- Can not comment and share on another person's diary
- Impossible to intervene in Facebook groups

The use of a professional facebook page has significant advantages to include in its customer acquisition strategy!

How to start and develop your presence on Facebook ?

The profile page is, in my opinion, the support to prioritize to start to be known on this social network. Facebook now favours posts from personal profiles on the newsfeed. The organic reach of the posts of a corporate page plummets, tumbles. It is mandatory to advertise for the chance to touch his fans on a corporate page. With a personal profile, it is much easier for a freelancer to create a community around what he has to share (other than commercial offers). With a personal profile, always in a spirit of sharing, freelance has the opportunity to gain visibility by also relaying its publications in Facebook groups. So I advise you to focus on your profile page to find your first contacts directly, to make you known, as a person and create a second time a pro page to federate around your brand and develop your business.

From this moment, two solutions are available to you:

- Turn your profile page into Pro page and get your friends who will become your fans.
- Create a Pro page to complement your profile.

I do not recommend the first solution, because all the content of your profile will be lost! The second solution is therefore preferred even if you have to invite your friends to like your Pro page. Anyway, those who will not accept your invitation are simply people who do not really care about you, your content! In a global way, wait until you have developed your traffic via other communication media before setting up your professional Facebook page.

How to succeed to make known on this social network ?

Coupled with a blog, Facebook is the ideal social network to share an article, create an event, announce the launch of a new training, react to your community and listen to it to understand its expectations. In addition, Facebook offers a favourable environment for a customer relationship with Messenger or the exchange of private messages. That said, we must not lose sight of the fact that social media is not a means of communication for direct selling.

So, there are "aggressive" methods on Facebook to avoid , and yet very often used. For example, many people ask me to be their friend via their profile and as soon as I accept the connection:

They ask me to like their Pro page.

Reaction: I look at it once in 10 Or again, I immediately receive a commercial offer by messenger.

Reaction: I avoid or even better, I get looped commercial offers via messenger.

Reaction: I delete the match.

To take full advantage of the viral effect of this social network, you will have to:

- Always be in a spirit of sharing. The more you spend your time doing your promo, the less you'll be visible.
- Publish quality content on your profile and / or your Facebook business page in line with the expectations of your readers.
- Be regular by creating and following a publication schedule. For example, you can schedule a different type of content for each day of the week.
- Invest in advertising campaigns (facebook ads);if necessary, create your own Facebook group.

Why choose LinkedIn this social network?

With 14 million users in France , LinkedIn allows any company to access groups of expertise, to find a contact or a company, to prospect and also to enhance its expertise through the sharing of information. LinkedIn specifically targets professionals . This media is not suitable for BtoC. LinkedIn is positioning itself as a true platform for publishing content and sharing information for companies:

- Lynda: tutorials and online training.
- Pulse application: publishing articles directly in LinkedIn

Choosing this social network is perfect if your goal is to develop your professional network, find BtoB clients and recruit new employees.

How to make yourself known on this social network?

Before asking someone to join your network, I strongly recommend that you engage with them:

- Leave a message (when possible) with your link request leave one or more comments on his publications share one or more of his posts.
- Prospecting on LinkedIn requires time and customization. There is no point in getting maximum contact if you have not bothered to introduce yourself intelligently.

Besides the fact that you have to look after the presentation of your profile (as for all social networks), you will also have to:

- To be regular in the publication of posts (articles, images, videos). Once a day minimum
- Write and publish articles directly on LinkedIn
- Interact with other members of your community
- Leave relevant comments to position you as an expert
- Share your knowledge in specific groups related to your field of activity
- Actively research and monitor important players in your industry
- Invest in their advertising program. Attention, it is difficult to obtain a return on investment.

Why choose Instagram as a social network?

Launched in 2010, Instagram is an exponentially growing social network with more than 14 million monthly active users in United states of America. It is also considered one of the best social networks in terms of commitment (number of shares and comments). Instagram is a visual-based application and many people (especially young people aged 18 to 24) like this type of publication, this proximity report where everyone can deliver a part of themselves through photos.

Although Instagram can be used in any industry, this social network is more attractive in market niches where photography is predominant such as: fashion, cooking, fitness, beauty, travel, art). Instagram advertising is integrated into the Facebook platform with many targeting possibilities. Choosing this social network can be a plus for your business, to communicate through the visual and create proximity to your audience.

How to be known on Instagram?

To take full advantage of the visibility of this social network, you will have to:

- Choose your theme: The chosen theme is the central core of your Intagram account. It is therefore important to choose it well.
- Present a coherent visual identity: The Instagram posts remaining displayed on your profile, you must harmonize the aesthetics of your publications. For example, you can add a filter to your photos to present a dominant colour on all your photos.
- Publish your visual experiences regularly: You have to publish beautiful visuals about your company, yourself, your team members or your customers. Post at least once a day and at the same time if possible.
- Use hashtags: By using appropriate hashtags, you will make your business more easily known to a large, targeted audience.
- To be active: You must "like" the publications related to your theme. And, of course, you always have to reply to your subscribers' messages.
- Track your results: It will analyse the results of your Instagram account to optimize your visibility and increase the number of commitments of your subscribers.

Did you know ?

> - A hashtag is a word that is written by putting a pound sign (#) at the beginning. (ex: #Mot)
> - It allows to group in a theme all that you publish on a social network such as Twitter, Facebook, Instagram. Using hashtags, your posts are potentially distributed to all users of the social network doing a search on the topic concerned (the word inserted in the hashtag). Otherwise, ie without the use of hashtags, your posts will be accessible only by your subscribers.

Why choose YouTube as a social network?

With more than 800 million unique visitors each month, this video platform has become the second largest search engine in the world, after Google. In addition, YouTube videos are well positioned in Google's search results. YouTube is the ideal social network to gain visibility with video content. YouTube should be seen as a channel for acquiring new visitors. If you get views only from readers of your blog or your existing prospects & customers, setting up this social network will have little interest to increase your visibility.

The goal is:

- Find topics to deal with that can get good SEO potential. For this, it is necessary to analyse the existing competition before choosing a theme to be treated in video.
- Create a series of quality videos and attract new visitors to its website & blog to convert them into prospects and customers.

How to make yourself known on YouTube?

The video is the support in vogue at the moment: it is visual and attractive. Nevertheless, the most difficult thing is to stand out by:

- Caring for the design of his chain; offering videos that have potential for sharing (video using emotion) or SEO positioning potential (series of tutorial videos).

In addition, each streaming setting for your video on YouTube needs to be optimized:

- Choose the right category for YouTubeInsert Tags , keywords that can bring you traffic.
- Choose the best encoding format possible: HD format.
- Make a nice screenshot with a title for the thumbnail of the video; insert "call to action" so that your visitors subscribe to your channel or go to your website.

Why choose Twitter as a social network?

With more than 20 million active users in United state of America, Twitter is a social network that will allow you to interact in real time with your followers (your subscribers) and publish news daily. His specialty: comment on the news in 280 characters, going to the basics.

The choice of this social network is interesting for:

- Information monitoring (follow experts and benefit from their expertise).
- Get in touch with influencers.

How to be known on Twitter?

Even if it is fast to create an account, you must know that to gain visibility on Twitter, you have to intervene several times a day and be followed by many people. The more you "tweet", the more likely you will be that your followers "Retweet" your information. On the lookout for the latest trends, Twitter users (bloggers and web specialists) are generally demanding on published news. This will require you to be precise and relevant on your watch so as not to jeopardize your e - reputation.

To develop your visibility on this social network, you will have to:

- Twitter information that interests your subscribers and not commercial offers use hashtags to increase the reach of your tweet.
- To measure the popularity of your hashtag on Twitter, you have this tool.

- Add an image or video to your tweet related to the subject of your tweet regularly (several times a day) to maintain the reputation of your company.
- Twitter at the right time by testing the hours that work best retwitter by making a relevant comment and adding a mention (@Automername) so that this retweet is visible to the subscribers of the author and for all your subscribers.
- Always thank your subscribers for their retweet conduct surveys to challenge your audience (your subscribers) interact with your community and follow the people you want to follow.
- Connect with influencers to become ambassadors for your brand stay yourself and always be in a spirit of sharing.

The more social network you have to really interact with people, the more visibility you will get: Facebook, Instagram, Twitter. It is certain that the ideal is to be placed on several social networks. But, do not forget, quality before quantity. Communicating on networks is very time-consuming, requires planning, and becomes uneconomical if misused. Your primary goal for communicating well on social media is to have your subscribers visit your blog by clicking on a link.

Whatever the social network chosen, it is imperative to:

- To fill his profile well; actually used the chosen social network.
- Develop and maintain a consistent editorial line.

The interest of these book is threefold:

- Convince yourself to use social media for your business, a strategic lever nowadays essential.
- Convince yourself that before embarking on this path, you need to plan a strategy, an editorial line and do not go head-on.
- Convince yourself not to disperse by starting with several social networks (initially choose a single social network is good enough for an independent.)

THE SECRETS OF AFFILIATE MARKETING

Wondering if affiliate marketing is a real business opportunity? Do you want to get started or improve your results? Want to avoid frequent mistakes and optimize your strategy? This guide unveils the keys to successful affiliate marketing. You too, become a smart affiliate! Are you new to affiliate marketing? Do you want to understand everything in a few minutes? I invite you to read beforehand: the operation of affiliate marketing. In affiliate marketing, you position yourself as an advertiser or an affiliate. In this article I will deal with the case where you are an affiliate, a partner willing to promote another person's products & service.

One must never forget that the fundamental principle of affiliate marketing is a "win-win" relationship. If you want your partners to promote your offers by affiliation, it is obvious that you will have to do the same for some of them.

- ➢ The smart affiliate distinguishes myths and reality.
- ➢ The smart affiliate does not commit these 5 mistakes.
- ➢ The smart affiliate has a value proposition.
- ➢ The smart affiliate has a promotion strategy

Myths and realities of affiliate marketing

Some think that affiliation only enriches advertisers. Others tried the experiment and only had disappointing results. So, is the marketing affiliation a real business opportunity or a disguised scam? To enlighten you, here are some distinctions between truths and received ideas.

1. **Affiliate marketing only enriches advertisers**

Fortunately for advertisers, very few deliberately mislead their affiliates. For an advertiser, affiliates are a sales force. The interest of an advertiser is to encourage, support, advise affiliates and not to deceive them.

How to detect a bad advertiser?

- A bad advertiser is not necessarily dishonest. In the vast majority of cases, when you do not earn commission, this is due to a tracking problem.
- By using a reliable affiliate platform such as Affilae, you will never have any problem in this regard.

- Do not work with advertisers who do not offer performance indicators: NB impressions, NB clicks.
- Do some testing with your affiliate link and see if a cookie is placed on your computer.
- For an advertiser who uses an internal affiliate program (eg WP affiliate plug-in) or a non-specialized external service, ask him for information about his tracking system, the duration of cookies.

2. **Promoting superlancing is always profitable**

Often, you will notice that the main partners of the advertiser (those who have large lists of contacts) offer many bonuses on the last day of the orchestrated launch. "If you want to get my bonuses, go through my affiliate link. " 99% of advertisers who perform superlays use a "last click" affiliate program.

It is therefore:

- The last affiliate who receives the commission
- One of the affiliates who offer the most bonuses

You understand. You did your job by sending all your prospects to the advertiser. And, you ultimately get very little or no sales. Because your contacts are part of the contacts of the big affiliates, partners of the advertiser. Unfortunately this affiliation commission theft by this process is very common, especially in the niche "earn money, live your dreams". So be careful. Promoting an orchestrated launch with a high commission is not necessarily profitable.

3. **I will make affiliate sales easily**

A lot of information circulates on the web presenting the affiliation as a quick and easy way to make money. It's wrong! The sale of an affiliate product, it learns and it takes time if you want good results. You will be told that it is possible to do affiliate marketing without having a website. For example, I notice that many do affiliation via social networks. The process itself is very simple. Examples:

You send a post to your contacts asking them to " type info " in comment if they want information. You answer them in MP by leaving your affiliate link.You comment on publications and leave your affiliate link in your response. Admit that this affiliate marketing process is rather dubious and aggressive. You will certainly (maybe) some sales easily, but sincerely it is not in this way that you will boost your incomes.

4. **The more affiliates who recommend a product, the more difficult it is to make sales.**

The number of affiliates is not the criterion to take into account. The real competition comes rather from "super affiliates", such as you if you apply the tips of this guide. The vast majority of affiliates are just putting a banner on their site. It is usually them who think that affiliation is not profitable. Others promote many products at once and never sell anything. "Super Affiliates" are those who focus on a small number of advertisers and deploy a real strategy.

5. **Cookies can be erased by visitors, so I can lose commissions.**

The cookie is the keystone of the tracking system of affiliate programs and therefore your remuneration as an affiliate. Even if the proportion of Internet users who deliberately delete their cookies is marginal, it should not be forgotten that some Internet users delete cookies from their computer.

Reminder: thanks to an innovative technology proposed by Affilae, each click is collected server side, and thus guarantees a continuity of tracking without cookie and by IP. In other words, even if a user deletes cookies from his computer, and he places an order, the commission will come back to you.

6. **95% of affiliates make few sales in affiliate marketing!**

Few affiliates make sales for four key reasons:

- They are not trained in affiliate marketing.

- They advertise banal, even aggressive.

- They sell, they do not advise.

- They do not know the product they sell.

7. **Some users do not like to click on affiliate links**

Internet users are often ready to put their hand in the purse to buy what interests them. But for strange reasons, they hate that an intermediary perceives a commission, even if it does not cost them a cent.

Why is it so important?

In general, when we speak of a Unique Value Proposition (PVU), we refer to the competitive advantages of a product. It's a connoted "marketing" term, but it has real meaning when you want to make sales in affiliate marketing. A value proposition is the set of benefits expected by a customer before paying for a product or service. Value is therefore above all a perception by the customer. As an affiliate, you're certainly not the only one promoting an advertiser's products and services, especially if their products or services are worthy of recommendation.

If you do not have a single value proposition to offer to your prospects, why would your prospects choose you over another? Why would they click on your affiliate link instead of another?

Example.

In 2010, I was doing affiliate marketing for SG-autoresponder and Aweber. I had more than 50 affiliates who took a subscription at home. Why ? I had a unique value proposition to offer them.

To stand out from the competition, you understand the importance of offering unique content to your readers. In affiliation, the competition is the other affiliates of the product or service promoted. Few affiliates make the effort to make unique content, write their own reminder letter, write an article. Of course, it is necessary to use the promotional tools provided by the advertiser, but it is imperative to put your added value without which your sales will be the drip.

How to bring your added value?

The foundation of success in affiliate marketing is to offer your prospects interesting content that they can not find elsewhere, and convey your personal experience in a sincere way. The best affiliates understand it. There is a well-known phrase that sums up the situation well: "20% of affiliates generate about 80% of sales or traffic on a site." Will you be in the 20%? The interest is not to take the place of the advertiser (the seller) by reproducing its sales page, listing for example all the benefits of the product. Your readers will expect you to tell them about your experience, to position yourself as an ally or advisor .

For example, if the affiliate product is:

A training

Present the objectives that it has allowed you to achieve, the skills that it has allowed you to acquire, the difficulties that you have overcome thanks to it and how, the qualities of the supports or the accompaniment, or more suggestions for improvement.

Software

Present a text or video tutorial on a specific use case. Write a user guide on how you use it. Write an article about its advantages and disadvantages and explain why you chose this product specifically. Make a comparison with other competing software that is to the advantage of the one you recommend.

A book, an ebook

Write a summary. Make a PowerPoint by commenting on elements that you particularly liked. Comment on the scope of the text and who it is for.

Whatever the affiliate product, you can also:

- Make a "testimonial" type video in addition to an article. Your message should remain informative and sincere. A testimony of complacency for the sole purpose of selling is always noticed. Offer a free guide that brings together many resources.
- Look for information, tips, and add-ons that are useful to your readers related to the Affiliate Product theme. Interview the advertiser. Talk to him about video recording an interview (on Skype or face camera) or writing an article on your blog. By obtaining this type of interview, you will increase the credibility of your recommendation.

Ideas to bring your added value are not lacking! It is up to you, at first, to build a knowledge base on the subject and product to recommend. It is only after this step that it becomes advisable to insert a link or an advertising banner of the advertiser on your website. But not before! As long as you have not offered free and unique content to your visitors objectively presenting the affiliate product, any advertising element inserted on your website will bring you very few results.

For example, if you promote an affiliate product solely for its high sales commission, without having tested it, you will not be able to convince your readers and your recommendations will lack credibility. Why ? Your prospects are not fooled. In the long run, you will surely lose their trust, the cornerstone of all relationships. In other words, think about your readers before thinking about your wallet, think above all to recommend only products that you know and appreciate.

The smart affiliate has a promotion strategy

Too often, affiliates leave without a clear and structured idea of the promotion strategy they will adopt. Yet nothing is more effective than methodical work. Here are two examples of simple and quick strategies to implement.

1. **Affiliate Marketing Strategy : Article + Affiliate Link**

Write an article on your blog with a compelling headline presenting the benefit of the affiliate product.

The body of the article should have several elements:

- Present in a few lines your tests, carried out successfully: why this product (software, training) can meet the needs of your readers (problem solved)?
- Describe the product, its objectives and its main benefits; Present your experience feedback, what it has brought you (positive points), the difficulties you have encountered (negative points);Finish your article with a call to action and your affiliate link.

This strategy works, but it has the disadvantage of sending your prospects directly to the seller's site . You no longer have the means to restart them.

2. Affiliate Marketing Strategy : Article + Affiliate Link + Gift

In the previous strategy, you do not have the ability to capture the email addresses of your prospects to relaunch them or to offer them other products on the same theme. In addition, as it is proven that a sale is generally made after several raises, there is a good chance that you will lose sales. It is therefore relevant to use a variant of the first strategy. In addition, you will end your article by inserting a registration form linked to your emailing service. By validating the form, your prospects will be listed on a contact list that you have created specifically for the promotion of this affiliate product. Thus, you have the opportunity to lead your prospect naturally in the sales process with a series of automated emails each having a specific objective.

This strategy is a balance between providing useful information and encouraging them to place an order through your affiliate link. By writing informative emails, you will be able to create a sense of reciprocity among your readers that can get them to support you by buying your recommendations. In order for this affiliate marketing strategy to be effective, your gift (guide, video, free training) must be quality and directly related to the affiliate product.

Instead of sending a simple email, it is advisable to:

- Write an article presenting your impressions and the result you have obtained;
- Create a useful gift for your prospects;
- Create a specific contact list to boost your prospects with useful and non-commercial information.

In conclusion: " Do not sell! Position yourself as a counselor." The product is ROI! You must pay attention to what you are going to advise. If you offer money, you will surely lose the trust of your customers. In this case, your customers will not be ready to choose another product in your "shop". Before recommending an affiliate product, here are three questions you should ask yourself:

- Is the product quality?
- Would I recommend this product to my family, my friends?

- Is the price of the product honest with the service provided?

If not, you may be able to make some money but your credibility will be very much compromised for the future.

Now you are informed!

Affiliate marketing is not and has never been a miracle recipe to boost your income. Like any marketing process that works in the long run, membership requires work, efficiency and ethics!

www.ingramcontent.com/pod-product-compliance
Lightning Source LLC
Chambersburg PA
CBHW080612220526
45466CB00010B/3322